EUROPEAN
AIRPORTS
Second Edition

ALAN.J.WRIGHT

IAN ALLAN
Publishing

Contents

Front cover picture supplied courtesy of NV Luchthaven Schipol.
Back cover supplied courtesy of Aer Lingus.
Previous page: a busy apron at Gatwick viewed from the centre pier. *AJW*

First published 1989
Second edition 1995
ISBN 0 7110 2334 4

Published by Ian Allan Publishing

an imprint of Ian Allan Ltd, Terminal House, Station Approach, Shepperton, Surrey TW17 8AS.
Printed by Ian Allan Printing Ltd, Coombelands House, Coombelands Lane, Addlestone, Weybridge, Surrey KT15 1HY.

Acknowledgements
Grateful thanks are extended to all the authorities that responded to the request for details of their airports. In some cases the wealth of information supplied was almost sufficient for a book in its own right. On the other hand, some failed to reply, but it is accepted that language barriers can prove difficult and may explain the silence. Of course, no replies would have been received without the efforts of the European mail services, whether operated by the traditional organisations or the courier companies. While the transit times varied considerably, almost all consignments arrived intact, with only two envelopes that plainly carried a request to remain bend-free being handled by a short-sighted official. The efforts of all concerned are much appreciated because without them there would have been no book.
Sincere thanks are also extended to British Airways AERAD for supplying the charts used for each airport. It must be remembered that these must NOT be used for operational purposes.

Introduction

The second edition of this book has been compiled with the co-operation of many of the airports consulted, albeit without the same degree of detail in all cases. It would appear that a number of authorities are reluctant to disclose facts and figures in case they are of value to potential visitors. Others obviously believe that security would be breached if details of the airport were revealed. The latter is, of course, a valid point, but the precautions should also be strictly maintained at the passenger checks at the entrance to the airside. Undoubtedly, peering at a TV monitor is a boring occupation and one that encourages a loss of concentration, yet at some airports there seems less enthusiasm for the checking of hand baggage for lethal weapons than for advising stationary observers to move from the boundary fence.

Fortunately, a number of authorities have recognised that there will always be visitors, so it is preferable to accommodate them in a suitable spot rather than clutter the surrounding roads with groups of spectators. Interestingly, the best facilities are those offered at major airports such as Düsseldorf, Frankfurt and Geneva, although in the UK, Manchester now has an excellent site on the perimeter. If no official viewing area is provided, then extreme caution should be exercised when venturing elsewhere. This is particularly relevant for those intent on photography, because the sight of a camera can cause great excitement amongst security staff. It also has to be remembered that many European sites are jointly operated by the military and civil authorities, which invariably means tighter security. While inside the police station, time can be spent pondering on the possible identity of likely aggressors now that Russia has been transferred to a friendly status. The question is unlikely to be answered, but the time spent inside the building could certainly be employed more pleasantly.

Inevitably, with the vast number of airfields and airports in Europe, space limitations alone have restricted the coverage in this volume. Therefore the first — and main — part is devoted to the larger airports of the various countries and those which attract a considerable volume of seasonal traffic. In the second part some of the quieter sites are recorded in less detail. At these locations it is usually much more likely that a request for permission to enter the airside will be granted without hesitation. It is also worth bearing in mind that the French nation is on holiday from mid-July until mid-August, which brings a severe cutback in domestic services.

As in the first edition, no attempt has been made to include costs, because with the exchange rate variations, devaluation, inflation and recessions, accurate figures would be impossible to record. In addition to being convenient for those wishing to fly, airports also provide the opportunity to change money because the banks located therein are usually open outside normal hours.

Aircraft types shown are those most likely to be used by the airline concerned, but of course these do vary from time to time depending on availability etc. Finally, it must be borne in mind that even where long-established facilities exist, there is always the risk that the authorities will suddenly remove them without warning for some reason. By using common sense and accepting the rules and regulations of the country, a most enjoyable and profitable time can be spent at most European airports.

Abbreviations

ABA	Aktiebolaget Aerotransport
ATI	Aero Trasporti Italiani
BA	British Airways
CDG	Charles de Gaulle
CSA	Ceskoslovenske Aerolinie (Czechoslovak Airlines)
DNL	Det Norske Luftfartselskap (Norwegian Airlines)
IT	Inclusive Tour
KLM	Koninklijke Luchtvaart Maatschappij (Royal Dutch Airlines)
LOT	Polskie Linie Lotnicze (Polish Airlines)
LTU	Lufttransport-Unternehmen
MD	McDonnell Douglas
MHz	Megahertz
OLT	Oltfriesische Lufttransport

Airport Codes

BRU	Brussels	GNB	Grenoble
BSL	Basle	GVA	Geneva
BVA	Beauvais	HAM	Hamburg (Fuhsbuttel)
CDG	Paris (Charles de Gaulle)	HEL	Helsinki
CFE	Clermont-Ferrand	IBZ	Ibiza
CGN	Cologne/Bonn	INN	Innsbruck
CMF	Chambéry	JER	Jersey
CPH	Copenhagen	LAZ	Lanzarote
DUB	Dublin	LGW	Gatwick
DUS	Düsseldorf	LHR	Heathrow
EBJ	Esbjerg	LIL	Lille
EIN	Eindhoven	LIN	Milan (Linate)
ETZ	Metz/Nancy	LIS	Lisbon
FBU	Oslo (Fornebu)	LPA	Las Palmas
FAO	Faro	LUX	Luxembourg
FCO	Rome (Fiumicino)	LYS	Lyon
FRA	Frankfurt	MAD	Madrid
FUE	Fuerteventura	MAH	Mahon
GLA	Glasgow	MAN	Manchester
		MLA	Malta
		MPV	Montpellier
		MRS	Marseille
		MST	Maastricht
		MUN	Munich
MXP	Milan (Malpensa)		
NCE	Nice		
ORY	Paris (Orly)		
OST	Ostend		
PGF	Perpignan		
PMI	Palma		
RHE	Reims		
RTM	Rotterdam		
SCN	Saarbrücken		
SNN	Shannon		
STR	Stuttgart		
SXB	Strasbourg		
SXF	Berlin (Schönefeld)		
SZG	Salzburg		
TFS	Tenerife (Reine Sofia)		
THF	Berlin (Tempelhof)		
TLS	Toulouse		
TUF	Tours		
TXL	Berlin (Tegel)		
VIE	Vienna		
ZRH	Zürich		

Above: Geneva's terrace is an excellent vantage point for shots of an Air Afrique DC-10, this example being TU-TAM. *A. S. Wright*

Top Right: Switzerland attracts a large number of executive aircraft, with Berne having its share of movements. Both prop and jet types are to be seen, Learjet 31 D-CSAP being one of the latter variety. *AJW*

Middle Right: Interot is one of a number of regional airlines that serve Berlin/Tempelhof, in this case Dash Eight D-BAGB is in service. *AJW*

Bottom Right: Malmö Aviation's BAe 146-200 SE-DRA taxying to its stand at Bromma. *AJW*

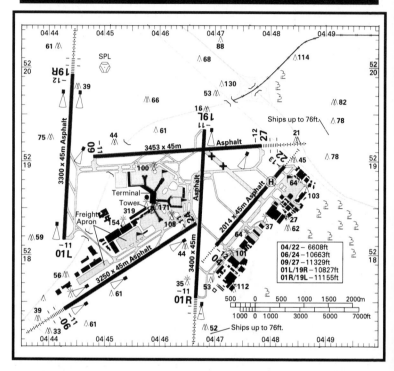

Amsterdam (Schiphol)

For a country so small, the Netherlands has always played a significant part in world affairs out of all proportion to its size. Much additional land has been reclaimed from the sea through the years, one such area being that now occupied by Schiphol. Haarlem Lake (Haalemmermeer) was a vast expanse of water which changed in shape and size at regular intervals. It covered 22,500 acres in 1250 but, as the banks were eroded by the wind-driven waves, by 1544 this figure had increased to 28,900 acres. There were considerable merchant shipping movements serving the town of Haarlem while ferries criss-crossed the lake, the dimensions of the boats dependent upon the locks built at the various exits. For good measure a naval battle was fought on 26 May 1573 between the Dutch and the Spanish fleets.

During the following years the lake steadily grew, until in 1836 it was decided that something must be done to halt the shrinking of the countryside, particularly since both Amsterdam and Leiden came under threat after a severe storm. By 1848 all was ready for the removal of the water by means of three steam-powered pumping stations, a task which took four years to complete and left the bed of the lake between 10 and 15ft (3-4.65m) below sea level. Unknown at the time, it was later to provide the base for an international airport which could then claim to be at a lower altitude than any other in the world.

Before this could happen, 50 years or so had to pass before the invention of the flying machine, plus a few more, before the first aeroplane actually landed on the site in August 1916. With World War 1 in full swing elsewhere, it was a military machine that

6

found the grass field conveniently close to the local Fort Schiphol, a Dutch army establishment. Subsequently an airfield was laid out, a feature which attracted the attention of several farsighted individuals.

One of these was Anthony Fokker, a Dutch national who just prior to the outbreak of war had built an aircraft factory at Mecklenburg, Germany. Some of the best designs were used with great success by the German Air Force, causing considerable problems for the Allies. Following the Armistice in 1918, Fokker wisely returned to his homeland with all speed accompanied by much useful liberated material and valuable expertise. Quick to appreciate the possibilities offered by civil aviation, he registered a new company in Amsterdam to embark immediately upon the design of the first of his range of airliners.

Another to recognise the potential of commercial air services was an ex-army officer named Albert Plesman. He managed to secure sufficient backing to form a new company which took the name Koninklijke Luchtvaart Maatschappij (KLM) in September 1919. Well aware of the attributes of Schiphol, not surprisingly Plesman selected the site for Amsterdam's civil terminal. By virtue of its origins, the area was completely flat, had no obstructions and embraced a more than adequate 190 acres of grassland.

International air services had been introduced by the British operator Aircraft Transport & Travel (AT&T) in August 1919 by making use of converted wartime machines. There was little alternative but to follow suit if KLM was to maintain its leading position. Still with no aircraft of its own, the company chartered the DH16 registered G-EALU from AT&T for the initial trip from Croydon to Amsterdam on 17 May 1920. Even in those days the weather was unhelpful, forcing the machine and its two pioneering passengers to cross the North Sea at an altitude of 300ft. After 2¼hr the DH16 became the first civil transport arrival at Schiphol, followed the next day by the new airport's inaugural departure when the same aircraft returned to the UK in equally appalling conditions.

Services gradually built up during the summer to provide links with several European cities, but on 31 October activities were suspended for the winter months as planned. The low-lying field was a haven for mists and fog which in 1920 presented unacceptable dangers. During the first five months of operations, 345 passengers had passed through and 48,500lb of cargo had been handled, a creditable achievement for such a new venture.

It was 14 April 1921 before the fledgling airport stirred itself again, but in the meantime KLM had ordered its own aircraft from Fokker with which the company was able to restart the London service. Ground facilities had been improved during the lull and on 25 August a cafe, hotel and restaurant were opened. Throughout the 1920s the number of flights from Schiphol increased to include a variety of long distance sorties. In fact when the regular schedule to Djakarta was introduced on 12 September 1929, the 8,540-mile trip became the world's longest route.

Schiphol was of course steadily developed in line with the increase in traffic. Concrete aprons were laid in front of the terminal buildings, which by the mid-1930s were far more substantial and to a modern design. The Fokker factory had also grown in size, especially after securing the European sales and manufacturing rights for the Douglas DC series. By 1938 the airport had expanded to cover 520 acres, becoming only the second in Europe to have paved runways. Scheduled services now accounted for 80 movements per day while passenger totals moved into five figures annually. Sadly this progress was destined to be abruptly halted with the advent of World War 2. Aircraft production at Schiphol in 1939 already concentrated on machines of a more aggressive nature, but their numbers were insufficient to offer anything other than token resistance when needed in 1940.

On 10 May it was Schiphol's turn to receive the full attention of the Luftwaffe. Eighteen airliners were destroyed by bombs which left Amsterdam's fine airport in a sorry state, with hangars and other buildings in ruins. While a certain amount of repair work was carried out for the unwelcome visitors during the occupation, the effort was of little value. Nevertheless the area received regular attention from Allied aircraft which added to the general destruction begun by the Germans. With the end of the dreadful period in sight, no hangars remained, all being wrecked or dismantled for transportation in pieces to less vulnerable sites. On the field Schiphol's runways were pitted with over 200 craters, effectively rendering them completely useless.

Despite these enormous problems, the Dutch workers enthusiastically filled holes and erected temporary sheds to allow the

Top Left:
One of United Airlines long-range Boeing 767s during turnround at Schiphol. *Amsterdam Airport Schiphol*

Left:
Swissair's Fokker 100 HB-IVA departs from Schiphol's Runway 01L. *Alan J. Wright (AJW)*

Bottom Left:
Martinair uses its 747s for long-haul freight work, with PH-MCE in service on this occasion. *AJW*

Above:
Transavia normally employs the 737-200 PH-TVH for its Amsterdam-Gatwick schedule, but a Series 300 is expected to take over in the near future. *AJW*

Below:
KLM Helicopters operate from Schiphol Oost. *AJW*

first postwar commercial movement on 28 July 1945, the distinction going to the Swedish airline ABA. Amazingly, the airport was ready for intercontinental operations on 28 November when a DC-4 resumed the five-day trek to Djakarta. Nearer home, European destinations were gradually reintroduced as the various terminals were made serviceable. On 21 May 1946 Schiphol became the departure point for the first scheduled postwar flight to New York, the KLM DC-4 calling at Prestwick and Gander *en route*. Although operational, the facilities at the Dutch airport were merely a temporary expedient until plans were agreed for its future. During the war years various schemes had been devised and these formed the basis for the reconstructed complex.

Originally, the proposed layout called for six runways arranged tangentially around the central terminal area. By the time approval was received for the project in October 1956, it was apparent that modern airliners were less concerned about wind direction than earlier types, so it was possible to reduce the total to four. At one point in the construction the main Amsterdam to The Hague road had to be rerouted to pass through two impressive tunnels under the newly laid operational area. Completion of the main runways did not come until 1968, which then gave Schiphol the full use of two pairs of almost parallel strips, plus a supplementary pair for the use of general aviation and Fokker. While all this work continued, passenger and freight traffic had been handled in the buildings reinstated after the war on the eastern perimeter. Woefully inadequate for many years, the opening of what was known as Schiphol Central in April 1967 came not a moment too soon.

This fine new structure possessed three piers equipped with airbridges, a feature not to be found on such a scale elsewhere in the world. Large as it seemed at the time, it was not long before expansion became necessary, which in due course led to the erection of a fourth pier. After its opening in 1975 no further major work was needed until the mid-1980s when an extensive programme of modernisation and development began which included the complete rebuilding of C pier (later renamed E). A brand new freight centre was also opened to accommodate the growing amount of cargo handled by the airport. This massive programme of improvements was known as Schiphol 2000 and designed

to meet the demands at the turn of the century.

Meanwhile there was every expectation that the passenger terminal's designed capacity figure of 16 million would be reached by 1989, so some form of relief was deemed necessary pending the completion of the airport's major expansion at the western end of the building. It was B pier (later D) which offered the best solution since sufficient space was available to construct an arm on its southern side. This enabled another 13 gates to be provided, thereby taking the total number of airbridge-equipped stands at Schiphol to 58. The pier will grow a similar arm on its northern side in the mid-1990s, but in the meantime the first section was duly opened by HRH Prince Bernhard of the Netherlands on 3 May 1990.

Although the development certainly helped loading and unloading, it was appreciated that the accommodation in the main terminal would begin to suffer strain under the extra pressure unless some action was taken. This threat was countered by the erection of a temporary extension at the southern end of the building. This short-term structure should be adequate until the first phase of the permanent replacement is completed.

Construction work on the latter project began towards the end of 1989 and added another 150m to the existing terminal. The enterprise will be completed in stages to keep ahead of demand, the initial section having entered service in May 1993. By this time the fifth pier was also ready, its presence adding another seven 747-400 stands plus one for an MD80. At this point Schiphol's capacity rose to 27 million passengers annually, which the authorities are confident will be sufficient to cater for growth until 1996. Conveniently, this will coincide with the completion of the second phase of the western extension.

When the entire exercise is finished in 2003, the airport will be large enough to handle 34 million travellers per year with six piers (B to G) protruding from the large single terminal. Outline plans have been made for a seventh pier, but if this becomes necessary it will have to be remotely situated on the far side of the nearby motorway. A high-level transit system would be installed to link it with the main unit. Similarly, within the greatly enlarged building some form of people-mover will be required because of the distances involved. Currently, Schiphol's minimum connecting time is 40min for European and 50min for intercontinental flights, but this is in danger of becoming unrealistic without the provision of fast internal transport.

Segregation of EU and non-EU passengers planned for 1996 has been taken into account. Virtually all services from the new West extension will be non-EU, while the southern departure hall will accommodate predominantly EU traffic plus the flights of Swissair, Austrian, Finnair, Istanbul Airlines and Turkish Airlines. Exceptions to this division are Martinair, which will move its entire operation to the West (EU and non-EU), plus Air Holland and Transavia, which will remain in the South Hall. KLM (including its partners Northwest and Air UK) will use Central, the renamed northern departure hall.

Early in the planning stages it was realised that as the piers increased in number, so it would become more difficult to monitor aircraft ground movements. A new tower was therefore commissioned so that an unobstructed view of all runways, taxiways and aprons would be possible. Construction of the 85m shaft began in April 1989 and took only 25 days to complete. When eventually handed over to the Dutch Civil Aviation Authority it had reached 94m in height and was ready for the installation of radar and associated electronic systems. When its radome was in position it had gained another 6m 41cm to give Schiphol the distinction of possessing the world's highest control tower.

By 1994 there was an impressive total of 23 routes linking the airport with the UK, over which 610,000 passengers were carried in the first six months of the year. Many of them used Schiphol as a transit point because of its excellent facilities, taking advantage of the growing number of connecting flights available. For many years regional carriers used a large apron beyond the main building with bus transfers for all passengers. This changed from 11 August 1994 when the newly-built B pier opened with the ability to handle 14 regional flights simultaneously with a maximum capacity of 1,400 passengers. It can accommodate both turboprops and jet types and incorporates airbridges as well as covered bus exits for easy access to the aircraft.

The airport's development plan has tried to reduce the number of houses in the vicinity that are affected by noise. Since aircraft movements will increase, this will only be possible with quieter types and a different pattern of runway usage, to be achieved by the construction of a fifth runway parallel to the existing 01L/19R. This will give Schiphol the capacity to handle the increasing traffic without delays, while at the same time contributing to a reduction in environmental pollution.

Altogether, the latest developments at Schiphol are most impressive. It was already one of the most pleasant airports to visit and the reception there is always friendly. However, a scheme designed to add to the general appeal may not meet with unanimous approval. The Authority has a 'green plan' for the surrounding landscape, one of the proposals being the planting of 63,000 trees. It is to be hoped that they are of the bonsai variety or do not proliferate around the perimeter, thereby spoiling the excellent views currently enjoyed!

Location and access: Situated 9.3 miles (15km) southwest of Amsterdam alongside the motorway connecting the city with The Hague and Rotterdam. Ample car parking with spectators directed to one particular area. Netherlands Railways links Schiphol directly with Amsterdam Central station with a journey time of 20min. Connections are available to a wide range of destinations. To the south the railway serves such places as Antwerp, Brussels and Rotterdam. Central Nederland Buses serves numerous districts surrounding the airport. Tickets purchased can be used on either or both forms of transport anywhere in the Netherlands.
Terminal: A large spacious building which contains a number of snack bars, restaurants and banks plus a large selection of shops. It is a long walk from one end of the terminal to the other.
Spectator facilities: An excellent terrace is provided along the front of the terminal building from which most movements can be seen. It is also a good spot for photography, with many of the arriving or departing aircraft taxiing past within range of a 200mm lens. An additional viewing gallery located on the west wing has now been opened, with access from Terminal South and Terminal West. Opening hours remain the same as the original facility — between 10.00 and 18.00 throughout the year. Excellent spots are to be found around the airport boundary, particularly alongside runways 06/24 and 01L/19R. The former can be reached by taking a bus to the village of Rozenburg followed by a walk to an official car park and viewing area. Ideally,

private transport is preferable but at least a mobile snack bar visits this otherwise remote spot. Unlike most other airports, much of the perimeter of Schiphol is marked by wide, toad-infested ditches, making the erection of 10ft-high fences unnecessary. Photography is therefore unimpeded. There is also an aircraft museum located in a dome-shaped building in the central area. Opened in 1971, the Aviodome contains about 30 airframes covering the history of aviation, particularly that relating to the Netherlands. Unfortunately, the lighting conditions within the structure do not favour the photographer, but there is a Grumman US-2N Tracker parked outside, albeit surrounded by shrubs. The museum is open daily from 10.00 to 17.00.

Operators: Aer Lingus (Boeing 737), Aeroflot (Tu-134/154), Affretair (DC-8), Air Engiadina (Dornier Do328), Air Exel Commuter (Brasilia), Air France (Airbus A320, Boeing 737, Fellowship, Brasilia, SAAB SF340), Air Holland (Boeing 757), Air Lanka (TriStar), Air Malta (Airbus A320, Avro RJ70, Boeing 737), Air Portugal (Airbus A320, Boeing 737), Air UK (BAe 146, Fokker 100, Fokker 50), Alitalia (MD80), Austrian Airlines (MD80), Balkan (Tu-154), Bangladesh Biman (DC-10), BASE Regional (Jetstream), British Airways (Boeing 737/757), British Midland (DC-9, Boeing 737, Fokker 70/100), Cathay Pacific (Boeing 747, Airbus A340), China Airlines (Boeing 747), Croatia Airlines (Boeing 737), Crossair (SAAB 340/2000), CSA Czechoslovak Airlines (Tu-134/154, Boeing 737), Cyprus Airways (Airbus A310/320), Delta Air Lines (Boeing 767, TriStar), EgyptAir (Airbus A300/320, Boeing 767), El Al (Boeing 747/757/767), Estonian Air (Tu-134), Euro Direct (Jetstream, ATP), Eurowings (ATR-42/72), Finnair (DC-9/10, MD80), Garuda (Boeing 747), Gulf Air (Boeing 767), Iberia (Airbus A320, Boeing 727/757, DC-9, MD80), Icelandair (Boeing 737/757), Iran Air (Boeing 747), Istanbul Airlines (Boeing 727/737), Japan Airlines (Boeing 747), KLM (Boeing 737/747/767, DC-10, MD11, Airbus A310, Fokker 100), KLM CityHopper (SAAB SF340, Fokker 50, Fellowship), Korean Airlines (Boeing 747), Kuwait Airlines (Airbus A300/310), Lithuanian Airlines (Boeing 737, Tu-134/154), LOT Polish Airlines (Boeing 737, Tu-134/154), Lufthansa (Airbus A320/321, Boeing 737, Fokker 50), Maersk Air (Boeing 737), Maersk Air UK (One-Eleven), Malev (Boeing 737, Tu-134/154), Martinair (Boeing 747/767, MD11), Malaysian Airlines (Boeing 747), Nippon Cargo Airlines (Boeing 747), Northwest Airlines (DC-10, Boeing 747), Olympic Airlines (Boeing 737), Palair Macedonia (Fokker 100), Pakistan International (Boeing 747), Regional Airlines (SAAB SF340, Jetstream), Riga Airlines Express (SAAB SF340), Royal Air Maroc (Boeing 727/737), Royal Jordanian (Airbus A310/320), SABENA (Boeing 737), SAS (DC-9, MD80), South African Airways (Boeing 747), Singapore Airlines (Boeing 747), Suckling Airways (Dornier Do228), Swissair (MD80, Fokker 100), Tarom (Boeing 737, One-Eleven, Tu-154), Thai Airways International (DC-10, MD11), TMA of Lebanon (Boeing 707), Trans World (Boeing 747/767), Transavia (Boeing 737/757), Tunis Air (Airbus A320, Boeing 727/737), Turkish Airlines (Airbus A310, Boeing 737), Tyrolean Airways (Dash Eight), Ukraine International (Boeing 737), United Airlines (Boeing 747/767), Varig (Boeing 747), Viasa (DC-10), Viva Air (Boeing 737), ZAS Airline of Egypt (Airbus A300, MD80).

Movements (1993): Total 287,938. Total passengers 21,274,407.

Runways: 01R/19L (11,155ft/3,400m), 01L/19R (10,827ft/3,300m), 09/27 (11,318ft/3,450m), 06/24 (10,662ft/3,250m), 04/22 (6,608ft/2,014m).

Radio frequencies: 118.1MHz, 118.9MHz (Tower), 119.05MHz (Departure), 121.8MHz (Apron), 121.975MHz (Approach).

Telephone: (020) 6012673 (Information)

Operated by: Schiphol Airport Authority

Athens (Hellenikon)

During the last 20 years or so Greece has steadily increased in popularity with European holidaymakers, with the consequence that Hellenikon has become a much busier airport. Opened in 1936, it was built on the coast with limited facilities and a fairly short strip to serve as a runway. Plans to develop the site were quickly put into effect in 1945, but five years later work was suspended until investigations had been completed into possible alternatives. Satisfied with the outcome, approval was given for the general enlargement of the airport, which involved the acquisition of large areas of land to the south and east. Part of the scheme called for a new international terminal to be constructed, thereby leaving the original single-storey building for the exclusive use of the national carrier, Olympic Airways.

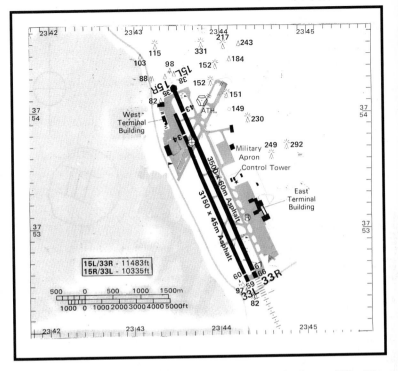

West Terminal Building

ATH.

Military Apron

Control Tower

East Terminal Building

350D x 60m Asphalt

3150 x 45m Asphalt

15L/33R - 11483ft
15R/33L - 10335ft

500   0   500   1000   1500m
1000 0 1000 2000 3000 4000 5000ft

Traffic continued to grow at such a pace that the new structure, opened in 1969, had to be extended in the mid-1970s to raise its capacity as the wide-bodied types came into service. These aircraft also needed additional space for parking, so the apron was increased in size to allow six 747s to be handled simultaneously. Nevertheless, Hellenikon's future depended upon it expanding still further and this was limited by the shortage of suitable land. Added to this handicap were the constant complaints from members of the local population about noise and pollution, so the government decided once again to seek other possible locations for a brand new Athens airport. Of the four sites studied, that at Spata-Saggani was the final choice for a complex capable of handling 15 million passengers when opened. Two parallel runways 13,000ft (3,962m) in length were envisaged, while the terminal area would contain three circular buildings each served by four triangular-shaped gate-lounges. In the meantime Hellenikon continues as the main gateway

to Greece, accounting for over 75% of the country's air traffic movements.

Location and access: Situated 6 miles (10km) south of Athens. The western terminal (Olympic) is served by a bus to the city centre (Avenue Syngrou 96), a journey of 20min. There is also a Yellow Bus service between the terminal and Piraeus (Akti Tzelepi, Karaiskaki Square). This bus includes a visit to the eastern terminal in its travels, a destination additionally served directly from Syntagma Square, the Blue Bus service taking 20min for the trip.
Terminals: The eastern building handles all except Olympic and is divided into two halves for arrivals and departures. Also within the building is a section dealing with charter movements. The western terminal is used by Olympic. There are no modern devices such as airbridges at either of the two terminals, buses taking all passengers to and from the stands.
Spectator facilities: There are virtually no viewing facilities remaining at the western

13

terminal occupied by Olympic. At the northern end there are windows which overlook the apron used by the flag carrier's training aircraft, but otherwise there is little reward for visiting this building. The international east terminal offers slightly better facilities. In the arrivals section, a lounge provides views over a portion of the active apron, with photography possible through the glass, bearing in mind the reflections and position of the sun. The roof of the departures building is still accessible, but with the useful part closed. This still leaves a restricted view of the apron with limited value for photography. As an alternative the airport perimeter offers better prospects, although stationary bodies by the threshold of Runway 33R inevitably attract the attention of unwelcome visitors. From the quantity of these prowling law officers, the profession appears to be the answer to the nation's unemployment problem. Since they are usually inflexible in their attitudes, discretion is undoubtedly wise in order to avoid a compulsory inspection of the interior of a police station. Nowadays, many visitors stay at the Hotel Emmantina, which regularly advertises its attractive position and amenities in the UK aviation press. In addition to being a good vantage point, it also offers the convenience of a pool, bar and refreshments on its rooftop terrace.

Operators: Aeroflot (IL-86), Air France (Airbus A300, Boeing 737), Air Malta (Avro RJ100, Boeing 737), Air Portugal (Boeing 737), Alitalia (MD80, DC-9, Airbus A300), Austrian (MD80), Balkan (Airbus A320, Boeing 737), Bangladesh Biman (DC-10), British Airways (Boeing 737/767), Condor (Boeing 737/757/767), CSA Czechoslovak Airlines (Tu-134, Boeing 737), Thai Airways International (Boeing 747), Cyprus Airways (One-Eleven, Airbus A320), Delta Air Lines (Airbus A310, Boeing 727/767), EgyptAir (Airbus A320), El Al (Boeing 737/757), Ethiopean Airlines (Boeing 757), Gulf Air (Airbus A320), Iberia (Airbus A320, Boeing 727/757), KLM (Boeing 737), Kuwait Airways (Airbus A310/320), LTU (MD11), LOT Polish Airlines (Boeing 737), Lufthansa (Airbus A300/310/320/321, Boeing 737), Luxair (Boeing 737), Malev (Boeing 737, Tu-154), Middle East Airlines (Boeing 707), Olympic Airways (Airbus A300, Boeing 727/737/747, ATR-42/72, Dornier Do228), Pakistan International (Airbus A310), Royal Jordanian (Boeing 727), SABENA (Boeing 737), SAS (MD80), Singapore Airlines (Boeing 747), South African Airways (Boeing 767), South East European (Fokker 50, Metro), Swissair (Airbus A310/321, MD80), Syrian Arab (Boeing 727), Tarom (One-Eleven, Boeing 737), Tunis Air (Airbus A320, Boeing 727/737), Turkish Airlines (Boeing 737, Avro RJ70), Trans World (Boeing 747), Ukraine International (Tu-134), United Airlines (Boeing 727, DC-10).

Movements (1993): Total 120,000. Total passengers 9,414,000.

Runways: 15L/33R (11,483ft/3,500m), 15R/33L (10,334ft/3,150m), 03/21 (6,000ft/1,828m). Normally only 15L/33R is used, the other two serving as taxiways or for aircraft storage.

Radio frequencies: 118.1MHz, 122.1MHz (Tower), 118.3MHz (Radar), 121.7MHz (Ground).

Telephone: (01) 9699111

Operated by: Civil Aviation Authority

Berlin/Tegel

Due to the difficulty in coping with the continuous stream of movements at Tempelhof during the Berlin airlift, some form of relief was urgently needed. The decision was taken to construct a new runway in the Jungfernheide, near Tegel, in the northern part of the city. At the time, its 7,874ft/2,400m length made it the longest in Europe, yet it was completed in only three months, an amazing achievement. Over 19,000 Berliners were employed in the levelling of the 300,00sq m site and the subsequent building operations. Although formally opened on 1 December 1948, a USAF C-54 became the first aircraft to land when it arrived on 5 November. When the blockade was lifted in the following October, there had been 277,728 movements shared by the three airports (Gatow being the third), with some 2,326,205 tonnes of supplies flown to the city.

Although Tegel had proved invaluable during this period, immediately the operation ended in 1949 there was very little activity for over a decade. However, as the airlines began to introduce larger types towards the end of the 1950s, it became apparent that the vast expanse of Tegel could be usefully revived. So on 2 January 1960 the appearance of an Air France Super Constellation marked the arrival of the first regular civilian traffic. Two weeks later the

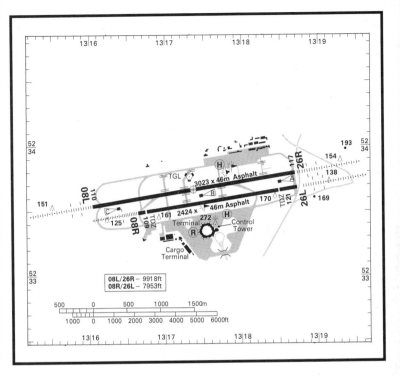

08L/26R – 9918ft
08R/26L – 7953ft

same company introduced the Caravelle and it was not long before all the French carrier's flights were maintained by this type.

Naturally, more sophisticated buildings were needed, and were duly provided, but passenger traffic to Berlin was rapidly increasing, which meant more and more interim measures before anything more permanent could become available. Work began on a complete reconstruction of the airport in June 1969, a task which continued until the official opening on 23 October 1974. Already the base of Air France, Dan-Air and Laker, in 1975 it was decreed that Tegel should also welcome the remainder of the carriers still operating from Tempelhof. The ruling caused some difficulties initially, because Tegel was conceived as an additional facility rather than a replacement for the older site. These problems were resolved in due course and Berlin now has an excellent airport well up to the customary German high standard.

Most of the nation's terminal designs

offer some originality, and that chosen for Tegel is no exception. Arranged in hexagonal form, the 620m-long structure is fitted with 14 airbridges, 10 fixed and four that swivel to allow use by wide-bodied types. For every pair of jetties there is an arrivals room complete with its own conveyor belt and customs facility. This admirable idea eliminates the need for central baggage handling and helps to reduce the number of items going astray. For those travelling in the opposite direction, each departure point again has its own passport and customs control point, a large waiting room and a duty-free shop. In the middle of the hexagon is a short-term parking area, which can reduce the walking distance involved from car to check-in to as little as 20m.

Interim measures to increase the annual capacity of the airport to seven million passengers are being introduced, but construction of a temporary terminal to cope with an additional two million has been stopped. No other plans for major development had been announced by the end of 1994.

Location and access: Situated 5 miles (8km) northwest of Berlin, to which it is connected by a network of multi-lane roads free of intersections. City Bus route 109 connects the city centre (Budapester Strasse) with the airport, taking 30min for the journey. Route 128 links the underground station (U-Bahn) on Kurt-Schumacher-Platz (U6) with Tegel.
Terminal: Connected to the front of the hexagonal structure is the main building, within which are located the various airlines' desks, a bank and the usual shops. On the upper floors most of the space is devoted to the offices of both carriers and the airport authority, but on the third level there is a restaurant capable of seating 340 people.
Spectator facilities: Tegel has the roof of the hexagonal terminal allocated as a viewing terrace, resulting in an excellent vantage point. The entrance is to the left of the main building and it is open between 10.00hrs and 19.00hrs daily for a small charge. Also parked on the roof are a few items from the Air Classik Collection, the actual types changing from time to time as the exhibits are moved to and from other locations.

Operators: Aeroflot (Tu-134/154), Aero Lloyd (MD80), Air Berlin (Boeing 737), Air Charter (Boeing 737), Air France (Boeing 737), Air Malta (Boeing 737), Air Portugal (Boeing 737), Alitalia (MD80), Austrian Airlines (MD80), British Airways (Boeing 737/757), Delta Air Lines (Airbus A310, Boeing 767), Deutsche BA (Boeing 737, Fokker 100), Condor (Boeing 737/757/767), Finnair (MD80), Germania (Boeing 737), Hapag-Lloyd (Airbus A310, Boeing 737), Iberia (MD80), Istanbul Airlines (Boeing 727/737), KLM (Boeing 737, Fokker 100), Lithuanian Airlines (Yak-42), Lufthansa (Airbus A300/310/320/321, Boeing 737), Olympic Airways (Boeing 737), Royal Jordanian (Airbus A310), Sun Express (Boeing 737), Swissair (MD80), Trans World (Boeing 767), Turkish Airlines (Airbus A310, Boeing 737), Ukraine International (Boeing 737), United Airlines (Boeing 727/747).
Movements (1993): Total 93,213. Total passengers 7,064,640.
Runways: 08L/26R (9,918ft/3,023m), 08R/26L (7,953ft/2,424m).
Radio frequencies: 118.7MHz, 119.7MHz (Tower), 119.3MHz, 132.65MHz (Departure), 121.75MHz (Ground).
Telephone: (030) 4101-1
Operated by: Berliner Flughafen-Gesellschaft mbH

Berlin (Tempelhof)

Located only four miles (6.5km) from the centre of Berlin, Tempelhof became one of the busiest airports in Europe between the wars. Regular services began on 8 October 1923 to link the city with Munich, although the terminal building was a wooden shed until more substantive premises were constructed. By the turn of the year, there had been 100 movements which had carried 159 passengers and 1,300kg of freight. Even these modest figures prompted the authorities to anticipate growth, so by the end of 1924 work began on an impressive project, including the erection of some of the largest and most modern hangars in Europe. During the 1930s, the traffic volume boosted the airport into the leading position among its contemporaries, a distinction which inspired the final plans for major development.

It was during this stage that Prof Ernst Sagebiel designed the famous curved terminal building, a magnificent structure years ahead of its time. Long before the advent of complicated airbridges, Tempelhof was given an enormous canopy

under which the airliners could park so that passengers remained dry whatever the weather. By 1938 much of the complex was ready for occupation, which helped to offset the difficulties in dealing with the 63,000 movements and 247,000 passengers recorded during the year. Scheduled services linked Berlin with over 70 cities worldwide, but naturally this rapid growth slowed appreciably at the outbreak of war. At this point, routes radiating from Tempelhof were reduced in number, but the German capital was still connected on a regular basis with many destinations in neutral, friendly or occupied countries. In fact, commercial flying did not really end until 1945.

A survey of the scene revealed that while the airport had suffered considerable damage during the many air raids, the new terminal had somehow managed to escape the full effects. Under the control of the US forces, the buildings were restored so that a few services could be introduced by American Overseas Airlines in 1947, thereby providing the first postwar air traffic at Tempelhof. Most of the passengers were foreign nationals because Germans still

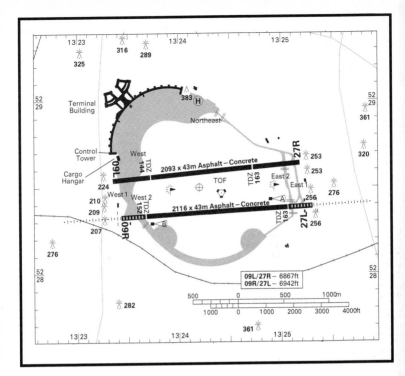

remained unpopular anywhere but in the Fatherland, always assuming they could obtain the necessary travel permits anyway. Suddenly, the fairly tranquil scene changed in June 1948 when the Soviet Union imposed a total blockade on West Berlin. There was only one solution — an airlift of supplies for the population. Consequently, the airport became one of the reception points, resulting in a constant flow of transport aircraft as they ferried the vital cargo from the west.

The operation lasted until 6 October 1949; the successful conclusion being marked in July 1951 by the unveiling of the Airlift Memorial on the Platz der Luftbrücke, the renamed square in front of the airport buildings. During the same year, some of the latter were handed over to the West German authorities so that commercial operations could be restored. Scheduled services were introduced by Air France, BEA, and Pan American, unexpectedly taking the number of passengers handled to 320,000 by the end of the first 12 months, a

figure which exceeded the prewar design capacity. Two years later the total had risen to 833,000, but fortunately the US released a further batch of buildings in 1959 which included the original departure/arrivals hall. By the early 1960s, Tempelhof had once again become an important centre, although it was 1964 before it received its first jet airliner, a Boeing 727 operated by Pan-Am. This type gradually replaced the carrier's DC-6B fleet in West Berlin, while BEA withdrew its Viscounts and Comets in favour of the One-Eleven.

With all this activity, it was plain that the airport had more than reached its ultimate capacity, even with the transfer of all charter traffic to Tegel in 1968. There was little alternative but to transform the latter so that it could also accommodate the scheduled flights. Consequently, on 1 November 1974, all commercial movements were moved to the newly-expanded facilities. Once again Tempelhof became much quieter, with the majority of the flying carried out by the USAF or US Army. In due course a few air

Top: Tempelhof's terminal retains an atmosphere from the past. *Berliner Flughafen Ges.mbH*

Centre: The famous curved terminal buildings and hangars front the extensive apron area. *Berliner Flughafen Ges.mbH*

Bottom: Airliners can park under the canopy for passengers to disembark at Tempelhof. *AJW*

taxi services were introduced, followed by limited commuter schedules in the 1980s.

The unification of Germany began a new era for the airport, helped in no small way by the reopening of the main hall in 1991. About a dozen regional airlines took advantage of the excellent amenities, although the equipment permitted was restricted to turboprops until the advent of Conti-Flug and the BAe 146. This company began a scheduled service to London City in October 1992, the route subsequently proving very popular with business travellers between the two cities. Shortly after the launch, the Canadair Regional Jet entered service with Lufthansa CityLine, the only other jet-powered type allowed into the compact airport. Nowadays it is surrounded by residential areas, which were largely responsible for the jet ban prior to the 146's introduction. These limitations also dismissed any thoughts of expansion, so the length of the parallel runways remain unchanged. Whether Tempelhof will eventually be completely closed remains to be seen, but if such a decision is taken to redevelop the city centre site, then Europe will have lost a valuable asset.

Location and access: Located four miles (6.5km) southeast of the centre and is served by U-Bahn 6 (Platz der Luftbrücke). Bus routes 104, 119, 184 and 241 also visit the airport from various parts of the city.
Terminal: The impressive marble concourse contains a few facilities, but it is mainly occupied by the various airlines' desks rather than the commercial activities normally found in airport terminals.
Spectator facilities: None provided, neither are there any vantage points near the terminal, so the only spots of use are at the ends of the runways. Some distance from the terminal a USAF C-47 and C-54 are exhibited in memory of the airlift, but neither are parked in a suitable position for a photograph through the substantial fence. If travelling, once through the security check it is possible to view the apron and view a few photographs of the aircraft on the near stands.
Operators: Berliner Spezialflug (Beech 1900), Croatia Airlines (ATR-42), Crossair (SAAB SF340), CSA Czechoslovak Airlines (ATR-72), Deutsche BA (SAAB SF340/2000), Eurowings (ATR-42/72), Hamburg Airlines (Dash Eight), Interot Airlines (Dash Eight, Beech 1900), Lufthansa (Fokker 50), OLT (Metro), SAS (Fokker 50), SABENA (Brasilia).
Movements (1993): Total 67,950. Total passengers 1,128,383.
Runways: 09L/27R (6,865ft/2,093m), 09R/27L (6,942ft/2,116m).
Radio frequencies: 122.1MHz (Tower), 119.3MHz, 132.65MHz (Departure), 121.9MHz (Ground).
Telephone: 6951-22 88/89
Operated by: Berliner Flughafen-Gesellschaft mbH

Brussels National (Zaventem)

When constructed after the war, Brussels' new airport was known as Melsbroek, the name of a nearby village. At this stage the terminal was situated at the northern side of the field, but plans for the future development of the site proposed a parallel runway layout with the main buildings between them. Work proceeded apace and the new passenger terminal was duly opened on 29 June 1958 to be renamed Brussels National. Initially two piers, each with eight gates, extended from the central block, although provision was made at the outset for more to be added when required. Unfortunately, fire destroyed much of the new accommodation in 1962, necessitating the use of temporary facilities until the rebuilt terminal was ready for use once again.

In 1973 a satellite spur was added towards the south, linked to the main area by an elevated walkway equipped with travelators. Airbridges were installed on this new circular extension, which was sufficient to contain the growth at the airport until the late 1980s. Land limitations restrict the ability to expand to some extent, but the first stages of a long-term development programme, designed to handle the forecast traffic in the early 21st century, are now under way.

The programme includes the provision of a new terminal building to the north of the existing structure, linked to A and B concourses. The latter is 2,132ft (650m) in length and will serve international flights, thereby replacing the two outdated finger piers. The second concourse is 1,312ft (400m) long and remote from the main building to which it is connected by a 1,115ft (340m) tunnel under the apron. It is

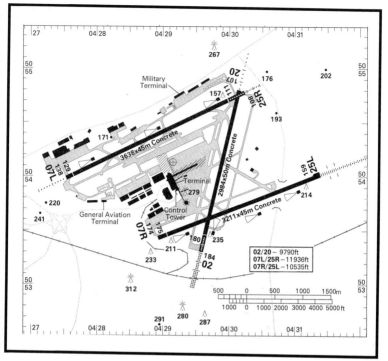

02/20	— 9790ft
07L/25R	— 11936ft
07R/25L	— 10535ft

due to be opened by 1999 to handle hub operations and is capable of expansion by up to a kilometre as business increases. Both concourses will have two levels and be equipped with airbridges, with departing and arriving passengers separated to improve both flow and security. A new railway station has also been constructed for the express train service into the city, while public road transport will benefit from a new bus station complete with an underground link to the terminal.

Part of the new facilities were expected to be opened in two stages during 1994, the first introducing two separate check-in and baggage claim areas to assist with the traditional holiday congestion. During this period it was planned that the old terminal would still be in use until the completion of stage 2 in November. At this point Phase 2 of the programme will be started which involves the refurbishment of the existing facilities and the provision of more gates. Nevertheless, it is planned that the airside departure areas will remain in use for flights

to EC destinations, leaving the landside section fully closed to the public. Work will continue on the remodelling of the building's departure area and gates until the end of the decade.

The entire complex will be served by the existing three runways which are considered to be adequate for the foreseeable future. However, an upgrading scheme was started in 1992 which involved the provision of parallel taxiways plus the addition of fast exits. Much of this work was completed to coincide with the opening of the new terminal, but some sections remain outstanding, particularly the apron area around Concourse A. The specification for the latter has yet to be finalised and will depend upon the type of traffic it will receive. While there is a remote possibility that a fourth runway could be built to the south, this is a very long-term prospect and would not be popular with the local population.

In common with all airports, Brussels has it share of professional protestors ready to oppose any developments. This includes night-flights, which since October 1991 have had landing fees charged according to which one of five categories is appropriate to a particular type of aircraft. The Authority does its best to reduce night-time noise by using procedures aimed at aircraft avoiding densely populated areas. Most of the movements are generated by the cargo services, but the efforts of the airport authority have proved effective, achieving a significant reduction in the number of flights between 23.00hrs and 05.00hrs. Ground noise has been contained by the erection of baffler walls around crucial parts of the airport and engine testing locations.

Some of the growth at Brussels has been created by the presence in the city of the administrative headquarters of the European Union, an organisation which became even more active after 1992. Another factor has been the airport's emergence in recent years as an important centre for air freight. A large cargo centre was built at the beginning of the 1980s which has since been responsible for the steady increase in tonnage handled. Chosen by Federal Express for its European hub, for some years the airport was regularly visited by the airline's DC-10s, while feeder services connected with the flights for the journey to and from the smaller distribution centres. However, in the early 1990s Fed Ex decided to reduce its European operation, moving out of its accommodation at Brussels in the process. This was duly taken over by DHL, which as a result has expanded its presence considerably.

Location and access: Situated 8 miles (13km) northeast of the city. Adjacent to the Brussels ring road and the interchange with the E10 motorway to Antwerp and beyond, the airport is easily reached by private or public transport. A rail link with the city's North and Central stations takes 14min and 18min respectively. SNCV bus route 578BZ from North station travels via Diegem, taking about 35min for the trip, whereas the 358 and 358B visit Woluwe on their way to the airport, which is reached after 45min. Other direct bus services are available from Antwerp, Ghent and Liege.

Terminal: Two buildings with Concourse B extending from the new terminal. All the usual facilities are available in the new complex with no access to the old terminal from the landside. Prices have always been high in the various buffets, so the new area

is unlikely to be any more attractive in this respect. Hopefully, the vast areas of glass will receive the attention of window cleaners on a more regular basis than hitherto.

Spectator facilities: None specifically provided nowadays. A number of aircraft stands can be seen through the glass overlooking the apron, but this restricted view is virtually useless for photography. There are several spots around the perimeter of the field which offer better prospects than anywhere in or near the terminal. One of these is by the threshold of 25L, which is reached from the village of Kortenburg, situated to the south of the airport. Good landing shots can be obtained here. Other spots exist near the thresholds of 25R and 02. Such vantage points may disappear in the near future due to the erection of earth banks and the planting of shrubs and trees in order to forestall any native uprisings against noise.

Operators: Scheduled services by Aeroflot (Tu-154, IL-86), Aer Lingus (Boeing 737, Fokker 50), Air Algerie (Boeing 737), Air Belgium (Boeing 737/757), Air France (Boeing 737), Air Malta (Airbus A320, Avro RJ70, Boeing 737), Air Mauritius (Boeing 767), Air Portugal (Airbus A320, Boeing 737), Air UK (BAe 146, Fokker 50/100), Air Zaïre (DC-10), Alitalia (MD80, DC-9), American Airlines (Boeing 767), Austrian Airlines (MD80), Balkan (Boeing 737/767, Tu-154), Brit Air (ATR-42, SAAB SF340), British Airways (Airbus A320, Boeing 737/757), British Midland (Boeing 737, DC-9, Fokker 100, Jetstream 41), China Eastern (MD11), Croatia Airlines (Boeing 737), Crossair (SAAB SF340), CSA Czechoslovak Airlines (Boeing 737), Cubana (IL-62), Cyprus Airways (Airbus A320), Delta Air Lines (Boeing 767, TriStar), Delta Air Transport (BAe 146, Brasilia, Fellowship), El Al (Boeing 737/757), EgyptAir (Airbus A320, Boeing 767), Euro Direct (ATP, Jetstream 31), Eurowings (ATR-42/72), Finnair (MD80), Garuda (Boeing 747), Iberia (Airbus A320, MD80), KLM (Boeing 737, Fokker 100), LOT Polish Airlines (Boeing 737), Lufthansa (Airbus A320/321, Canadair Regional Jet, Fokker 50), Luxair (Brasilia), Maersk Air (Fokker 50), Malaysian Airlines (Boeing 747), Malev (Boeing 737), Manx (Jetstream 41), Middle East Airlines (Airbus A310, Boeing 707), OLT (Metro), Olympic Airways (Boeing 737), Portugalia (Fokker 100), Regional Airlines (SAAB SF340), Royal Air Maroc (Boeing 727/737), Royal Jordanian (Airbus A310), SABENA (Airbus A310/340, Boeing 737/747, DC-10), SAS (DC-9, MD80),

Left:
An American Airlines DC-10 and Singapore Airlines Boeing 747 during their turnround at Brussels. *Brussels International Airport*

Below left:
A newcomer to Brussels in May 1994 was the newly-delivered Airbus A330 EI-DUB, at the time on an Aer Lingus proving flight. *Brussels International Airport*

Schreiner Airways (Dash Eight), Singapore Airlines (Boeing 747), Swissair (Fokker 100, MD80), Tarom (Airbus A310, One-Eleven), TAT (Fellowship), Thai Airways International (MD11), Trans World (Boeing 767), Tunis Air (Airbus A320, Boeing 737), Turkish Airlines (Airbus A310, Boeing 737), Ukraine International (Boeing 737), United Airlines (Boeing 767) and VASP (MD11). **Charter and IT operators:** Air Belgium (Boeing 737/757), Air Club International (Airbus A310), Air Europa (Boeing 737), Air Liberte (MD80), Air Transat (TriStar), Braathens (Boeing 737), Delta Air Transport (Fellowship), EuroBelgian Airlines (Boeing 737), European Airlines (Airbus A300, Boeing 737), Istanbul Airlines (Boeing 727/737), Onur Air (Airbus A320), Palair Macedonian (Fellowship, Fokker 100), Pegasus Airlines (Boeing 737), Royal Air (TriStar), Skyjet (DC-10), Sobelair (Boeing 737/767), Spanair (Boeing 767, MD80), Tyrolean Airways (Dash Eight). **Cargo operators:** Air Hong Kong (Boeing 747), Air Algerie (Boeing 737), China Eastern (MD11), DHL (DC-8), European Air Transport (Boeing 727, Convair 580, Metro), Fred Olsen (Electra), Gulf Air (Boeing 757), Hunting (Boeing 727, Electra), Saudia (Boeing 747, DC-8), Tunis Air (Boeing 737).
Movements (1993): Total 210,880. Total passengers 10,233,000.
Runways: 07L/25R (11,936ft/3,638m), 07R/25L (10,535ft/3,211m), 02/20 (9,970ft/2,984m).
Radio frequencies: 118.6MHz (Tower), 127.15MHz (Departure), 121.875MHz (Ground).
Telephone: (02)-7536800
Operated by: National Airways Company

Cologne/Bonn

Aviation received enthusiastic support in Germany from the very early days, with many cities anxious to be associated with this new form of transport. Consequently, when the first Zeppelin airship cruised over Cologne on 9 August 1909 it caused considerable excitement, resulting in the local officials seeking an agreement with the operating company, Deutschen Luftschiffahrts, to ensure that the city was included in the airship's services. Nevertheless, there were problems to overcome because the military authorities objected to the slow-moving machines passing over the district.

Progress could not be halted, however, and in 1911 the city announced its plans for the construction of a permanent airfield at Butzweilerhof. On 15 September 1912 the land was leased to the military, but the change did not mean an end to the site's aviation connection. In fact, after a grass strip was prepared and various buildings

erected, units of Fleigerbataillon 3 moved into what was now an airfield. When the war began both ground and air crew were trained at the base, an occupation which ended with the signing of the Armistice in November 1918. For the next few years Butzweilerhof was in the hands of the British Army of Occupation, but at last the troops departed on 1 January 1926 allowing the city to take over the airfield for development.

Within a short time there were regular flights between Cologne and destinations in Britain, France and Switzerland in sufficient numbers to justify expansion. On 23 April 1935 a start was made on the construction of new buildings, which duly became ready for operations about one year later, in July 1936. By the standards of the day, Cologne now had a world-class airport, attracting more than half of all the aircraft movements in the Rhineland-Westphalia region. As an international centre, it tied with Berlin as the second largest in Germany, Frankfurt taking the premier position.

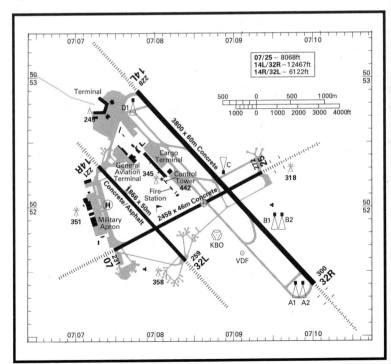

Once again war interrupted Cologne's progress and later occupation forces took control as they had done many years before. For some reason the city was excluded from the immediate postwar aviation expansion, but during the late 1940s it became necessary to reconsider the district's economic situation. Links with national and international markets were essential so the city's officials began negotiations to win approval for an airport to serve both Cologne and the newly-created federal capital at Bonn. Eventually the Civil Aviation Board of the occupying forces issued a licence for the combined use of Wahn by the two cities. Before the war the area had been an artillery range, but in 1938 it was converted into an airfield for the Luftwaffe, and its operators, until taken over by the Allies in 1945, whereupon it became an active RAF fighter base.

Initially, consent had been given for only one year, which did not give a great deal of security. Although the administration of the fledgling airport passed into German hands on 1 February 1951, development was halted early in 1952 when once again the facilities reverted to British control. This situation lasted until 1957 when finally, on 18 July, the site was handed over for the use of civil aviation. Being associated with Bonn meant that many international movements could be expected, so a programme of improvements was begun in 1958 to allow the airport to handle the largest of the new range of airliners then coming into service. By the mid-1960s traffic was outgrowing the terminal capacity, resulting in the construction of a new building which was eventually opened on 20 March 1970.

An interesting design was chosen to incorporate several novel features. Instead of one large hall for the completion of formalities, passengers pass directly to one of two star-shaped satellites each containing six gates complete with their own check-in desk. Even the main six-storey building succeeds in avoiding the rectangular box arrangement so often found. Instead, each floor is stepped back to given an attractive sloping effect, a design continued by the two angled side wings, although these have only four levels. By avoiding the conventional layouts at the planning stage, Cologne/Bonn has made the arrival and departure processes much easier for travellers. It also has the benefit of keeping aircraft turnaround times to a minimum since everything is accomplished

as close as possible to the appropriate gate. Due allowance was made in the early stages for future expansion when the traffic exceeded the 3.5 million-passenger capacity of the airport. Two additional satellites will be built and connected to the two side wings of the terminal, but this point has still to be reached. However, this may be achieved earlier than anticipated if some services are diverted from Düsseldorf in order to relieve the latter's busier facilities.

In addition to the airport's civil activities, the Luftwaffe's transport fleet is also in evidence here. Germany now has an enviable selection of airports built to imaginative designs for practical efficiency and appearance, Cologne/Bonn certainly maintaining the trend.

Location and access: Situated 11 miles (17km) southeast of Cologne and 17 miles (27km) north of Bonn with a direct spur from the motorway linking the two cities. Car parks are arranged conveniently for each level of the terminal. Express bus route 170 runs regularly from Cologne Central Station with a journey time of 20min. It takes 35min for bus service 670 to travel from Bonn Main station to the airport, a trip undertaken every 20min.

Terminal: Shops and refreshment facilities are located on both levels, all being within easy reach.

Spectator facilities: An open-air terrace extending along the front of the building has been much reduced in size to leave only a small area available at the end. From this often congested vantage point it is possible to photograph aircraft on the apron, but this view is also possible from within the terminal, a spot which is less crowded although fronted by tinted glass. Ideally, Runway 14L needs to be in use to justify a visit because all taxying traffic then passes the main building.

Operators: Aeroflot (Tu-154), Aero Lloyd (MD80), Air France (ATR-42), Alitalia (ATR-42), British Airways (Boeing 757), Cologne Air Transport (Titan), Condor (Boeing 757/767), Deutsche BA (Boeing 737, Fokker 100), El Al (Boeing 757), Germania (Boeing 737), Hapag-Lloyd (Airbus A310, Boeing 737), Interot Airways (Beech 1900), Istanbul Airlines (Boeing 737), Lauda Air (Canadair Regional Jet), LTE (Boeing 757), LTU (Boeing 757), LOT Polish Airlines (ATR-72), Lufthansa (Airbus A310/320, Boeing 737, ATR-42, Fokker 50, Canadair Regional Jet), Malev (Tu-134), Portugalia (Fokker 100), TNT (BAe 146), Turkish Airlines (Airbus

A310, Boeing 727/737), United Parcels (DC-8, Boeing 747).
Movements (1993): Total 100,200. Total passengers 3,775,000.
Runways: 14L/32R (12,467ft/3,800m), 14R/32L (6,122ft/1,866m), 07/25

(8,068ft/2,459m).
Radio frequencies: 124.975MHz, 120.5MHz (Tower), 120.25MHz (Approach), 121.05MHz (Radar), 121.85MHz (Ground).
Telephone: (2203) 400
Operated by: Flughafen Koln/Bonn GmbH

Copenhagen (Kastrup)

A field only a mile or so from Copenhagen's Town Hall Square was used as an aerodrome in the days before World War 1. Located at Klovermarken near Christianhavn, the rudimentary facilities served both military and civil flying needs until the 1920s. Even by the beginning of that decade the authorities had become resigned to the fact that the site was too small and that another location was needed for a new airport. Some farmland in Kastrup on the east side of the island of Amager was considered satisfactory for the purpose, especially since it also lent itself to the operation of

both flying boats and airships.

On 20 April 1925 Kastrup was opened to become the world's first exclusively civil airport. An interesting terminal building was constructed entirely of wood with a red tiled roof, quickly becoming known as the 'wooden castle' or 'summer house'. The latter was particularly appropriate because flying normally only took place during the summer months and even then was restricted to the spells of fine weather conditions. As intended, a quay was provided for waterborne machines although its use was strictly limited. Between 1925 and 1932 the build-up of traffic was gradual, but from this point until the outbreak of World War 2 there

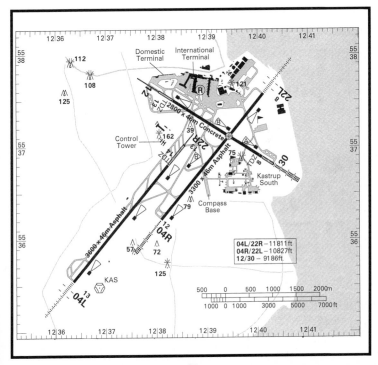

was a sharp upturn in movements. From a total of 6,000 in the early 1930s, by 1939 the figure had risen to 50,000.

As early as 1936 it became obvious to the planners that the airport was too small, especially since it had become the focal point for aviation in northern Europe. Consequently following a design competition, a brand-new terminal was built in time for opening in April 1939. Unfortunately it was barely a year later that the Germans took possession, although a small number of civil movements continued on routes to Sweden, Berlin and Vienna. During this period a concrete strip some 4,600ft (1,400m) long was laid to become the airport's first hard runway. Before the end of the war another three had joined this pioneer, a system of taxiways ensuring that Kastrup was a fully up-to-date international centre when the occupation ended in 1945. Fortunately the airport had suffered little damage, so it was soon ready for the new challenges.

Transatlantic services were started in 1946 by the newly formed Scandinavian Airlines System, thereby helping to boost traffic still further. Kastrup had become the third busiest airport in Europe by 1947, achieving a figure of 280,000 passengers per year. Terminal extensions kept the construction industry busy, because no sooner was one project completed than it was inadequate. One of the most ambitious programmes was begun in 1956 with lengthened runways, an entirely new terminal and numerous other improvements incorporating modern technology. It all restored Copenhagen's airport as the most advanced in Europe. Nevertheless it was necessary to construct two separate terminals later in the 1960s: one for domestic use in 1969 and the second to serve as an arrivals hall from 1971. Another runway was also laid parallel to 04/22 to permit simultaneous landings and take-offs, which had already risen to 180,000 per year despite the use of larger aircraft types.

Throughout the 1970s there was no further expansion because plans were already well advanced for the construction of a new airport on the island of Saltholm to the east of Amager. Before a start could be made on its construction, a committee was set up to investigate the merits of the project which by now appeared to be somewhat unnecessary in view of the traffic figures being appreciably lower than forecast. As is often the case, the scheme was therefore suspended indefinitely, with Kastrup remaining the international airport for Denmark's capital city. There was no need to alter the runway system, which was quite capable of coping with even the expected 22 million passengers in the year 2000. Extensions to the buildings were also straightforward, so the conclusion was that it was far cheaper to retain the well-established facility rather than spend an astronomical sum on the conversion of an uninhabited island.

Accordingly, work started on a modernised transit hall during 1982/83, followed in the next two years by the rebuilding of pier C to make it suitable for the handling of wide-bodied aircraft. Financial restraints created a delay in the programme, but eventually a new pier B was constructed in the 1980s, while 1989 saw a new domestic terminal and the expansion of parking facilities. Useful improvements were made on the landside by redesigning the road system, the surrounds becoming the home for numerous shrubs and trees during a planting spree. Elsewhere a new cargo centre began to take shape on the eastern perimeter in 1989, which was joined by two other units for DHL and SAS in 1992.

The next major project involves the construction of a new Pier A, to be joined in the second half of the 1990s by Pier D, a second international departure area and modern baggage sorting equipment. Towards the end of the decade a station will be provided to give access to the main rail system, thereby linking the airport with Norway and Sweden and the Jutland peninsula. When operational, the latest addition to the network will enable rapid and flexible connections to be made with the whole Nordic region.

Location and access: Situated 5 miles (8km) southeast of Copenhagen. A shuttle bus links the terminal with the city centre (Central Station) every 15min. There are 12 other public bus routes including Hovedstadens Trafikselskab bus route 32, which runs from the city centre to the airport in a journey time of 30min. A direct rail link is to be provided in the future.

Terminal: There are 18 restaurants, buffets and bars shared by the two terminals. Also within the complex are 30 shops plus the usual banks and service centres.

Spectator facilities: Another airport that possesses a long-closed roof terrace. In this case there are no real alternatives and very little can be seen of airside activities unless one is a passenger. Once through the security checks, there are numerous spots for viewing and photography available, so an early check-in is sensible. Away from the terminal complex, an excellent vantage point exists within the grounds of a cafe, although a 45min walk is required. It is reached by bearing left from the airport along the main road until the first access. At this point another left turn followed by more walking will eventually produce the welcome sight of the refreshment emporium. It is suitable for viewing or photography. While many of the movements are carried out by SAS, those of the Scandinavian charter companies such as Maersk, and Premiair Sterling also contribute to the statistics.

Operators: Aer Lingus (Boeing 737), Aeroflot (Tu-134/154, IL-62), Air China (Boeing 747), Air France (Airbus A320, Boeing 737), Air Portugal (Boeing 737), Air UK (BAe 146, Fokker 100), Alitalia (DC-9, MD80), Atlantic Airways (BAe 146), Austrian Airlines (MD80), Balkan (TU-134/154), British Airways (Boeing 737/757), British Midland (Fokker 100), Cimber Air (ATR-42), Croatia Airlines (Boeing 737), CSA Czechoslovak Airlines (Tu-134/154), Delta Air Lines (TriStar, Boeing 767), EgyptAir (Boeing 767), El Al (Boeing 747/757/767), Estonian Air (Boeing 737, Tu-134), Finnair (DC-9, MD80), Greenlandair (Dash Seven), Iberia (DC-9, MD80, Boeing 727/757, Airbus A320), Icelandair (Boeing 737), Kenya Airways (Boeing 757), KLM (Airbus A310, Boeing 737), Latvian Airlines (Tu-134/154), Lithuanian Airlines (Boeing 737, Yak-42), LOT Polish Airlines (Boeing 737, Tu-134/154), Lufthansa (Airbus A320, Boeing 737, Fokker 50), Luxair (Fokker 50), Maersk Air (Boeing 737, Fokker 50), Maersk Air UK (One-Eleven), Malev (Boeing 737), Middle East Airlines (Airbus A310, Boeing 707), Mukair (Bandeirante, Short SD3-30/3-60), Olympic Airways (Boeing 737-3), Pakistan International (Boeing 747), Palair Macedonian (Fokker 100), Royal Air Maroc (Boeing 737), SABENA (Boeing 737), SAS (DC-9, MD80, Fokker 50, Boeing 767), Singapore Airlines (Boeing 747), Sun-Air (Jetstream), Swissair (MD80, Fokker 100), Syrian Arab (Boeing 727), Tarom (One-Eleven, Boeing 737, Tu-154), TAT (Fellowship, Fokker 100), Thai Airways International (Boeing 747, MD-11), Tunis Air (Boeing 737), Turkish Airlines (Boeing 737), Varig (Boeing 747), Wideroe Norsk Air (Dash Eight). **Charter and IT carriers** include Air Liberte, Air Ops, Balkan, Canada 3000, Eurocypria, Maersk Air, Nordic East, Premiair, Spanair, Tarom and Transwede. **Cargo airlines** include Hunting, Maersk Air, Fred Olsen, Lufthansa, European Air Transport/DHL, Singapore Airlines and Mukair.

Movements (1993): Total 221,570. Total passengers 12,883,967.

Runways: 04L/22R (11,811ft/3,600m), 04R/22L (10,827ft/3,300m), 12/30 (9,186ft/2,800m).

Radio frequencies: 118.1MHz, 118.575MHz, 119.9MHz, 121.6MHz (Tower), 119.8MHz (Approach), 120.25MHz (Departure), 121.9MHz (Apron).

Telephone: 45 32 31 32 31

Operated by: Copenhagen Airports Authority

Dublin (Collinstown)

In the early days of commercial flying, the military airfield at Baldonnell, situated some 14 miles from Dublin, was employed for the limited number of movements by the small capacity airliners. Supposedly a temporary expedient, nevertheless very little serious effort was made to find an alternative until the launch of Aer Lingus in 1936. There was then more urgency, so site investigations were undertaken, one of those short-listed being the area previously used by the Royal Flying Corps/Royal Air Force at Collinstown. This had been one of four airfields chosen to become Training Depot Stations during World War 1, but the end of the conflict was in sight before the base was ready for its intended role. Collinstown continued to house token RAF units for some years until the final withdrawal of the forces from Ireland at the end of 1922. Thereafter the facilities were allowed to deteriorate gently until 1931 when Irish Aviation was formed with the intention of operating internal flights from the airfield, mainly with mail and newspapers. This enterprise did not last beyond the end of the year, so once again Collinstown was left to its own devices.

Finally, on 9 December 1936, the government announced that it proposed to develop the derelict airfield as Dublin's new civil airport. When the plans were released it could be seen that all of the existing dilapidated military buildings were to be demolished to make way for the terminal, hangars and other accommodation. Probably one of the main factors to influence the decision was Collinstown's

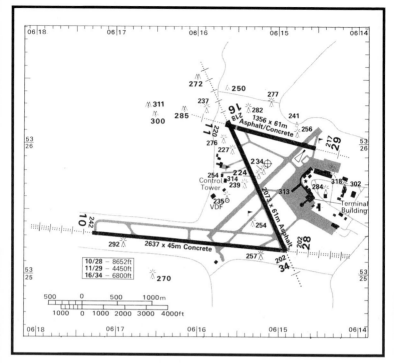

excellent weather record and its obstacle-free position 10 miles from the nearest mountains. Four grass strips were prepared, the longest being 5,250ft (1,600m), but although a few test flights were undertaken by the military in October, it was over two years later before the buildings were completed, the official opening taking place on 19 January 1940.

Dublin's new airport was then generally considered to possess the most impressive terminal in Europe. Designed by 25-year-old Desmond Fitzgerald, it had won him the award of a gold medal from the Royal Institute of the Architects of Ireland. Sadly few travellers could appreciate the building's excellence as the number of routes plied were now in the singular. Aer Lingus managed to maintain the link with Merseyside by using its DH86s or the newly acquired DC-3, intended as the basis for a modern fleet. Luckily this had just managed to evade the German forces as they advanced on Amsterdam, where it was being prepared for delivery by Fokker.

Otherwise it would undoubtedly have been destined for a career with the Luftwaffe had it survived the aerial attacks.

With the war at an end, the rapid increase in aircraft movements and size made a hard runway layout essential if the airport was to be able to handle the newer types successfully. Consequently three concrete strips were laid, the longest stretching for over 5,000ft (1,524m) and completed in 1950. As forecast, traffic steadily increased, until by 1950 over 150,000 passengers were using Dublin annually. Throughout the decade it was necessary to continue this programme of expansion, which meant new hangars were built and those existing thoroughly modernised.

In 1957 the launch of scheduled services by British European Airways, BKS and Sabena brought the time nearer when the terminal would need some attention. This point was reached during the next year because by now the national carrier had begun transatlantic services, a development which helped to ensure that the new North Terminal was opened on 8 June 1959 as an arrivals area. By this time the jet-age was looming, so once again both runways were extended until by the end of the next decade Dublin's two main strips had grown to 6,800ft and 7,500ft in readiness for the imminent arrival of the first of the latest monsters, the 747.

An enormous increase in cargo tonnage in the early 1970s led to the construction of a new freight centre to cope with nearly 40,000 tonnes per year. Passenger figures were now exceeding 1.6 million annually so inevitably yet another terminal complex was opened in 1972, this time capable of handling 4 million travellers. Very little growth was apparent in the 1980-85 period at Dublin, where the airport regularly recorded a throughput of some 2.6 million passengers. However with the advent of greater competition, particularly on the London routes, numbers climbed to 2.9 million in 1986 and over 3.5 million in the next year. This impressive performance not only represented an additional 600,000 passengers or a 20% increase on 1986, but an amazing 1 million greater than 1985.

Such an influx demanded some general reorganisation of the terminal arrangements, including a passageway to link the main departures area with Pier A in an effort to ease congestion. A more important development for the airport was the provision of the brand-new Runway 10/28. This was duly opened on 21 June 1989, but in fact the first official departure did not take place until eight days later, the distinction going to the Aer Lingus Commuter Fokker 50, EI-FKB. The introduction of the new strip allowed resurfacing work to proceed elsewhere and the general upgrade of the landing aids to begin. Eventually it was possible to relegate Runway 05/23 to taxiway standard.

In the early 1990s it was estimated that the annual passenger throughput at Dublin will reach seven million by the end of the decade. To meet this demand, an extensive development plan was devised to include terminal expansion, new passenger and cargo handling facilities and an increased area for public car parking. There will also be runway lengthening and further apron construction, the latter in readiness for a third pier on the cargo side of the main building. In the meantime, work started on the upgrade of Pier A in February 1994 which will include the provision of additional boarding lounges, together with the move of

the duty-free shop and customer service desks. During the winter of 1994/95 travelators were due to be installed in the Link building.

Location and access: Situated 5.5 miles (8.8km) north of the city off N1. A coach operates between the airport and Central Bus Station running every 20-35min with a journey time of 25min. Taking 35-40min for a similar trip, a variety of Dublin City buses visit the airport in their travels, some of which find their way to the city centre (Eden Quay). These are considerably cheaper, if somewhat slower, but the time can be spent pondering why one-man-operated buses have a conductor.

Terminals: These contain an excellent restaurant, plus self-service snack bars. A selection of shops provide for those with immediate requirements including anyone anxious to acquire a new tie. There is a security checkpoint on the approach road to the buildings.

Spectator facilities: A viewing gallery exists in the main terminal which affords good views of the proceedings, although photography is not entirely satisfactory through the tinted glass. Nevertheless, it is by no means impossible with care. As an alternative, the nearby multi-storey car park serves as a good vantage point, but of course security precautions may encourage the police to evict casual onlookers. At the end of the walkway between the main terminal and Pier A a small area lends itself for viewing the activity on this apron and the movements along the near taxiway. Photography is possible, but this time it is through untinted glass usually liberally decorated with finger marks. A similar handicap is experienced when using the usefully positioned windows in the main terminal. These overlook the stands on the east side of Pier B and are convenient for obtaining the occasional shot. Several good vantage points also exist around the perimeter adjacent to the thresholds of Runways 16 and 11, and these have the advantage of offering fresh air and no glass.

Operators: Aer Lingus (Airbus A330, Boeing 737/747, SAAB SF340, Fokker 50), Aeroflot (Tu-134), Aero Lloyd (MD80), Air Charter (Boeing 737), Air Columbus (Boeing 737), Air Europa (Boeing 737/757), Air Inter (Airbus A300/320), Air Malta (Airbus A320, Avro RJ70, Boeing 737), Air Portugal (TriStar), Air South West (Navajo), Alitalia (DC-9, MD80), ATS Vulcan (Bandeirante), British Airways (Boeing 737), British Midland

(Boeing 737), Channel Express (Electra), CityFlyer Express (ATR-42/72, Short SD3-60), CityJet (BAe 146), Crossair (BAe 146), Delta Air Lines (TriStar), Iberia (Airbus A320), Lufthansa (Airbus A320, Boeing 737, Canadair Regional Jet), Manx Airlines (ATP, Jetstream 41, BAe 146), Royal Airlines (TriStar), Ryanair (Boeing 737), SAS (MD80), TransLift (Airbus A320), TNT (BAe 146), Viva Air (Boeing 737).

Movements (1993): Total 90,200. Total passengers 5,905,000.
Runways: 10/28 (8,652ft/2,637m), 11/29 (4,450ft/1,356m), 16/34 (6,800ft/2,073m).
Radio frequencies: 118.6MHz (Tower), 121.1MHz (Approach), 128.0MHz (Radar), 121.8MHz (Ground).
Telephone: (01) 8444900
Operated by: Aer Rianta-Irish Airports

Düsseldorf (Rhine-Ruhr)

With the opening of Düsseldorf's airport on 19 April 1927, Deutsche Luft Hansa introduced scheduled services on routes within Germany to link the city with Berlin and Hamburg plus an international sector to Geneva. It was not the district's first contact with aviation because as early as 19 September 1909 Zeppelin airship Z.III landed on Golzheimer Heath, an area later destined to become a base for such devices. During the 12 years to the outbreak of war in 1939, expansion was at a leisurely

pace as reflected in the relatively modest passenger total of 87,333 recorded in this period. It was not surprising that civil flying was suspended at the outbreak of war, the airfield becoming the scene of military movements for the duration. No longer featuring in the timetables of the civil operators, it did however appear as one of the chosen targets for the RAF throughout the war, the frequency of the visits increasing by 1943. More accurate bombing was possible when the Pathfinder Force was introduced, both Mosquitos and Lancasters marking the target areas for the Main Force.

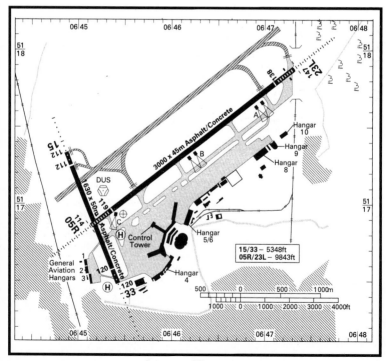

Left:
LTU's new MD11s are now to be seen at Düsseldorf, this example being D-AERW. *Flughafen Düsseldorf*

Bottom left:
Düsseldorf handles a considerable volume of charter traffic, some of it generated by Aero Lloyd's MD83 D-ALLQ. *AJW*

and France, by which time work had started on the construction of Runway 06/24, the future main 3,700ft/1,128m runway. Until 1 December 1950 control had been vested with the Allied administration, but on this date a new company (Düsseldorfer Flughafen-betriebsgesellschaft) was formed by the city and the State of North Rhine-Westphalia to take over the responsibility for the complex.

One of the heaviest attacks took place on the night of 2-3 November 1944 when 992 bombers were despatched to the city with great effect. Finally the entire complex was destroyed during a series of air raids on 23 December.

Reconstruction was slow to begin, but in 1948 a temporary terminal was provided and a makeshift 3,937ft/1,200m runway (17/35) was laid using steel plates. This method had been perfected during the war when there was a need for rapid completion of landing grounds. Scheduled flights were resumed on 4 April 1949 when British European Airways introduced a service from Northolt including both Hamburg and Düsseldorf in its journey, while SAS started to fly between the latter and Copenhagen. These carriers were quickly joined by Sabena, KLM and Air France to link the airport with the capitals of Belgium, Holland

At the beginning of the 1950s a permanent runway was laid to replace 17/35, the new strip becoming 16/34 and 4,750ft/1,450m in length. In those days aircraft were not as tolerant of crosswinds as they are now so it was necessary to provide something suitable. With this requirement no longer so important, nowadays its use is restricted to aircraft with a maximum weight of 8 tonnes. While this was in progress 06/34 was being lengthened to 8,100ft/2,475m and the airport also gained taxiways and additional apron area. When the postwar Lufthansa began operations in April 1955, Düsseldorf was already developing as one of Germany's major air transport centres, a role in which it has continued through the years. Nevertheless expansion was not too rapid in the 1950s but by the next decade the need for an enlarged terminal was becoming apparent. It was to be 1967 before the design was finalised and two years later before work actually began. Planned to be undertaken in stages, the first phase was completed in 1973 to allow the new Terminal 2 to be opened for operations. It brought immediate relief but was still only an interim solution pending the completion of the second phase in early 1977, Düsseldorf's 50th anniversary year, which was duly celebrated on 19 April.

While the single main runway was able to cope with the steady growth, a plan to build a parallel strip was accepted by a committee on 3 October 1976. The project evaluation procedure was instigated in the following June, but it was 16 December 1983 before the scheme eventually received approval and another seven years before a start was made on the construction of the new runway. It was formally completed on 2 September 1992, but was not opened to traffic pending the result of a number of court cases.

Throughout this time the original terminal had remained in service, but in 1982 work started on its replacement by providing another extension to Terminal 2 complete with the brand new Pier C. When opened in 1986, a total of 28 airbridges were available on the stands, many capable of handling wide-bodied types. Certainly there was less need to use buses between the building and the aircraft. Handling 13.1 million passengers in 1993, Düsseldorf is now Germany's second largest airport, with its traffic shared equally between scheduled and charter services. In fact, the airport is now the nation's leading centre for air-tourism. About 18% of the passenger volume originates from around the city. North Rhine-Westphalia accounts for a further 68%, these travellers coming mainly from neighbouring centres such as Essen, Duisburg, Bochum, Wuppertal, Krefeld, etc. Only some 14% travel from outside this region, many of them residents from the eastern fringes of Holland. It is often quicker to use the German airport than to travel to Schiphol, but much depends upon the ultimate destination.

According to the current forecasts for the aviation industry, the growth in demand is expected to increase the annual traffic figures to about 16 million passengers by the year 2000. To meet this challenge the Düsseldorf authorities have continued the programme of expansion with a main terminal building extension to produce more

convenient handling for both airlines and passengers alike. There are also plans to link the airport to the Federal German Railways' Intercity network featuring a special terminal with its own check-in facilities. The first phase of the new freight centre was due to open in November 1994 to boost the airport's annual throughput to 150,000 tonnes. This will be increased by another 25,000 tonnes in mid-1997 when phase 2 is opened.

Surface access has been considerably improved following the opening of the new A44 link with the autobahns to the east and west of the city. Such was the relief that the inauguration ceremonies continued for three days in October 1992!

The future of the airport is also largely dependent upon its environmental compatability. A soundproof hangar capable of housing a 747 was built exclusively for ground running jet engines, a necessary practice but one which generates strong complaints. Once the building was completed in September 1990, tests showed that there was an appreciable reduction in noise when compared with the level reached with the previous protection barriers.

It is possible that some of the regional flights will be relocated at nearby Mönchengladbach, thereby easing the load on Düsseldorf. This may also extend to the general aviation traffic, which, although having its own dedicated terminal on the southwest side, frequently shares the runway with the commercial movements. Similarly, more collaboration is planned with Cologne/Bonn in an attempt to streamline the air transport services in the North Rhine-Westphalia region.

Location and access: Situated 4 miles (6.5km) north of Düsseldorf it is well signposted from the nearby autobahns. Fast local trains on line S7 of the Rhine/Ruhr S-Bahn network connect the airport terminal to Düsseldorf Central station and Solingen-Ohligs, while S21 visits all important cities in the Ruhr region. Rheinbahn bus route 727 plies between the airport, Düsseldorf Central station and Tannenhof, while other buses provide direct services to Essen (route 153), Ratingen (760) and Krefeld (072).

Terminal: Departures are handled on the upper floor, arrivals at ground level, with the urban railway station below. Numerous shops, restaurants, cafeterias and snack bars are located around the building. There are three piers: A has 11 passenger airbridges, B has 9 while C is equipped with 8. All have an additional gate from which buses convey passengers to more distant stands. An extension to the central terminal was opened in May 1994 to be known as the Central East Building. Its position provides departing passengers with easier access from the parallel A44 motorway, especially those travelling with Lufthansa.

Spectator facilities: An excellent observation deck has been provided on the roof of Pier B with opening times between 06.00hrs and 21.00hrs. This is close to the taxiways so photography is no problem, a wide-angle lens often being useful. For take-off shots on the main runway a 200mm telephoto lens is required. The interesting Air Classik museum collection has now been dispersed to other locations.

Operators: Adria Airways (DC-9, MD80), Aer Lingus (Boeing 737), Aeroflot (Tu-134/154), Aero Lloyd (MD80), Air Alfa (Boeing 737), Air Berlin (Boeing 737), Air Canada (Boeing 767), Air Europa (Boeing 737/757), Air France (ATR-42, Airbus A320, Boeing 737), Air Liberte (MD80), Air Malta (Airbus A320, Boeing 737), Air UK (BAe 146, Fokker 100), Albatross Airlines (Boeing 737), Alitalia (DC-9), American Airlines (Boeing 767), Austrian Airlines (MD-80), Aviompex (Yak-42), Balkan (Tu-154), Birgenair (Boeing 737, DC-8), British Airways (Boeing 737/757), Canada 3000 (Boeing 757), Centennial (MD80), CityFlyer Express (ATR-42), Condor (Boeing 757/767, DC-10), Croatia Airlines (Boeing 737), Crossair (Fokker 50, SAAB SF340), CSA Czechoslovak Airlines (ATR-42, Boeing 737), Deutsche BA (Boeing 737, Fokker 100, SAAB SF340), EgyptAir (Airbus A320), Eurocypria Airlines (Airbus A320), Eurowings (ATR-42/72, BAe 146), Finnair (MD80), Futura (Boeing 737), Germania (Boeing 737), Ghana Airways (DC-10), Greenair (Tu-154), Hapag-Lloyd (Airbus A310, Boeing 737), Iberia (Airbus A320, Boeing 757, DC-9, MD80), Interot Airways (Dash Eight), Istanbul Airlines (Boeing 727/737), Japan Airlines (Boeing 747), KLM (Boeing 737, Fokker 50/100, SAAB SF340), LTU (Boeing 757/767, TriStar, MD11), Lufthansa (Airbus A300/310/320/321/340, Boeing 737/747, DC-10, Fokker 50, Canadair Regional Jet), LOT Polish Airlines (ATR-42), Luxair (Fokker 50), Meta Aviotransport (Yak-42), Oasis (MD80), Olympic Airways (Boeing 737), Onur Air (Airbus A320), Palair Macedonia (Fokker 100, Tu-154), Pegasus (Boeing 737), Rheinland Air Services (Cessna 425, Short SD3-60), Romavia (One-Eleven), Royal Air Maroc (Boeing 727), SAS (DC-9, MD-80), SABENA (Dash Eight, Brasilia), Sobelair (Boeing 737), Spanair (MD80), Sun Express (Boeing 737), Swissair (MD80, Fokker 100), Tarom (One-Eleven), Transavia (Boeing 737), Tunis Air (Airbus A320, Boeing 737), TUR European Airways (Boeing 727), Turkish Airlines (Airbus A310, Boeing 737), Tunis Air (Airbus A320, Boeing 727/737), Tyrolean (Dash Eight), Venus Air (MD80), Viva Air (Boeing 737).

Movements (1993): Total 155,596 (scheduled 116,948, charter 34,044). Total passengers 12,922,219.

Runways: 05R/23L (9,840ft/3,000m), 05L/23R (8,858ft/2,700m), 15/33 (5,348ft/1,630m).

Radio frequencies: 118.3MHz (Tower), 119.4MHz (Approach), 121.9MHz (Ground).

Telephone: 0211 4211

Operated by: Flughafen Düsseldorf GmbH

Frankfurt Main

Aviation was introduced to Frankfurt as early as 1909 when an International Air Show was staged. Hardly up to modern standards the main participant was indeed 'air', but it did mark the start of the city's involvement in flying which has continued to the present day. Two years later an aero club was formed in the locality at Rebstock from where commercial flights were introduced after the war. Such was the growth that in 1934 4,620 departures were recorded which accounted for 33,400 passengers, 552 tons of freight and 86 tons of mail. Already the total capacity had been reached and with no room to expand, approval was given to build a new airport on 300ha of forest land to the southwest of the city. In addition to the operation of fixed wing machines, facilities were included so that airships could be handled with ease. As a result, transatlantic services began in May 1936 using LZ127 *Graf Zeppelin* and LZ129 *Hindenburg*, but the violent end of the latter at the US Lakehurst terminal brought an abrupt end to such activities. In the meantime, Lufthansa had launched its services with a Junkers Ju52, an event which quickly multiplied to take Frankfurt into the position of Germany's second most important airport after Berlin/Tempelhof.

By this stage the site had more than doubled in size, so it was considered that the time had come for a Master Plan to be devised. In those early days, aircraft

Top: Frankfurt is still served by Adria's DC-9 S5-ABG. *AJW*

Bottom: Lufthansa's 747 D-ABZF handles some of the freight movements at Frankfurt. *AJW*

preferred to operate into the wind, so no hard runways were deemed necessary. This reasoning lasted until 1942 when a second scheme was produced by the authorities. Four concrete strips were now proposed, all to be laid at bearings decided after careful analysis of meteorological data collected over a lengthy period at nearby Rebstock. The southern boundary was earmarked as the location of all buildings, an area previously occupied by the airship facility.

Strangely, the latter's two hangers had already been blown up in May 1940 on the express orders of Herman Göring, Commander-in-Chief of the Luftwaffe. If he had waited, no doubt the task would have been satisfactorily carried out by the Allies. Needless to say, the 1942 plan

failed to come to fruition, but at least a hard runway was laid in 1943 for the use of the transport and fighter units based at the prewar airport. Unfortunately, it did not survive for very long because of its popularity as a target for bomb aimers. Finally, it was almost totally destroyed during two particularly heavy raids on Christmas Eve 1944 and 12 March 1945. While Frankfurt's career had effectively ended for the remainder of the war, at least the rubble produced was useful for the foundations of the new runway.

Reconstruction work became the responsibility of the Supreme Commander of the Allied Forces, with enough progress made by 14 August 1946 to give Danish Airlines (DDL) the distinction of operating the first postwar

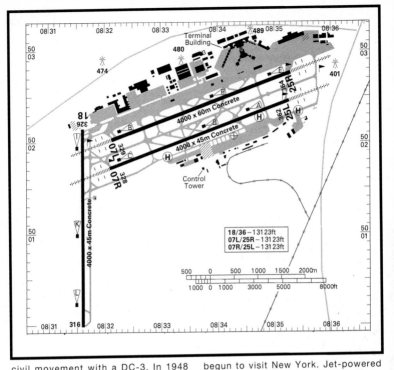

civil movement with a DC-3. In 1948 Frankfurt played an important role in the support of the aircraft taking part in Operation 'Planefare', the relief of besieged Berlin. Such was the intensity of the movements by the heavily-laden transports employed on the airlift that the runway became seriously damaged. As a consequence a second parallel strip was laid in 1949 whereupon the control of the airport was transferred to a German company. Still the scene of considerable military activity by USAF transports, the southern side was devoted to such operations while the northern area was allocated to the growing commercial activities.

It was almost 10 years after the war before the reborn Lufthansa was allowed to recommence flying, its first service employing one of four Convair 240s (D-ACAD) for a domestic sector on 1 April 1955. Two weeks later international services began and by the year's end not only was Frankfurt linked with most of the European capitals, but Super Constellations had

begun to visit New York. Jet-powered airliners were introduced to the airport on a regular basis in 1958 when BOAC Comets began to stage through on their way to Tokyo, but it was 1960 before Lufthansa's new Boeing 707s arrived to take over the daily transatlantic runs. In common with many other airports, Frankfurt's traffic increased dramatically until in 1965 4,875,850 passengers were handled. Once again the design capacity was being exceeded thereby demanding urgent expansion. Much planning work had already been completed on what was to become a massive new terminal so it was possible to lay the foundation stone in June 1965. It took six years of intensive activity by day and night to complete the building by which time its size had been doubled in anticipation of the arrival of the wide-bodied types. Finally, on 16 March 1972, operations were transferred from the original complex much to the relief of all concerned. Construction of a third runway (18/36) designed exclusively for take-offs was started in 1981, opening for traffic on

12 April 1984.

Frankfurt is the engineering base for the Lufthansa German Cargo Services and Condor fleets and also the flag carrier's largest international connecting point. Boeing 747s are maintained in a custom-built hangar capable of housing six of the type while another almost as large caters for the needs of DC-10s and Boeing 737s. Accommodation built much earlier is used for the other narrow-bodied airliners. From the beginning, the importance of air cargo was recognised so a freight centre was established on the western perimeter with warehouses capable of storing containers of all sizes. As a result the airport handles a vast quantity of freight, 70% of which is actually in transit. In recent years the growth rate has been much less than anticipated due in part to the difficulty of obtaining slots and the fact that landing and handling fees are higher than at competitive airports. Therefore while dedicated cargo aircraft are still to be seen, 94% of the total cargo tonnage in 1990 was carried on scheduled flights. In addition each night the airport plays its part in Germany's mail system, although the modest growth recorded is related to domestic traffic. Airmail on the European routes has been declining for several years, trucks taking over to save costs and to ensure punctual delivery.

Despite the somewhat disappointing figures in the early 1990s, the overall trend is for the demand in air transport to grow rapidly. The traffic projections for the year 2000 prepared by the Frankfurt authorities in 1985 had already been exceeded after only four years, so an urgent revision of the airport's future expansion plan was required. As an interim expedient a number of measures were introduced to create more space within the existing buildings, but the most significant feature was the new East Terminal, later known as Terminal 2. Opened in October 1994, it will eventually have the capability to handle between 10 and 12 million travellers annually, with a rapid transit system connecting the two complexes for easy interlining. Initially, some six million passengers will use the new accommodation mainly for intercontinental flights, because the building was designed for the larger aircraft expected early next century. However, since the plans were finalised, airlines have tended to use twins for long-haul work, so the provision of the extra space could be somewhat premature. Ultimately it is intended that by the end of the decade both terminals will be joined to bring everything under one roof once again.

Once this stage has been completed, after the turn of the century, Pier A will be extended southwards to provide four extra gates. All of this additional traffic will continue to use the three runways currently available, although a number of improvements will be necessary. More fast exits and taxiways are to be provided, but any plans to lay a fourth strip have been dropped. Undoubtedly Frankfurt will be well placed to meet the demands of the single European market and the liberalisation of air traffic when this programme is completed.

Location and access: Situated 5.6 miles (9km) southwest of Frankfurt at the Frankfurter Kreuz, the intersection of the A3 and A5 autobahns. There is a rail station under the terminal which is served by frequent trains. Line S15 connects with Frankfurt Central track 21 at 10min intervals, taking 11min for the journey, while Line S14 runs every 20min between Wiesbaden, Mainz, Russelheim, the airport, Central station and Konstablerwache. There are also intercity trains which link some 47 cities all over Germany. For the more adventurous a number of suburban buses visit the terminal. There are 15 stops numbered 10 to 24 allocated to the local routes that serve Morfelden-Walldorf, Kelsterbach, Bad Homburg, Darmstadt, Dietzerback, Dreieich, Russelsheim, Offenbach, Neu-Isenburg, Frankfurt-Sud and Frankfurt-Schwanheim.
Terminal: Contains not only restaurants and buffets but over 100 shops covering a wide range of services. For entertainment those not impressed by aircraft can make use of the skittles alley or visit the cinema.
Spectator facilities: Against all modern trends Frankfurt possesses a superb observation deck which is certainly one of the best in Europe and is open from 1 April until 30 September between 08.00hrs and 21.00hrs, closing time for the other six months being 18.00hrs. Access is gained from the gallery on the departures concourse of Hall A. A strict security checkpoint has to be passed before entry to the roof is permitted and this can take some time if carrying the normal equipment essential for enthusiasts. Once cleared, there is an impressive area available for spectators, although building work brought a reduction in 1994. Naturally a considerable number of Lufthansa aircraft parade before the onlooker at some time or other, but for variety the left side of Pier B offers excellent views of the charter traffic, some of which is not often seen in the UK. With the terminal facing south, sunny days can present a few problems for

photographers, but by taking up a suitable position this can usually be overcome. There are refreshment facilities on the roof but prices are high making it more economic to acquire food and drink in the basement supermarket. Fortunately, re-entry to the terrace is permitted, making sorties into the terminal quite practical and worthwhile especially since the TV monitors not only give arrivals and departures as customary but also the registration of the aircraft on the service. The admission charge includes the Historic Aircraft Collection which contains up to 20 exhibits. Airport tours, previously available for groups only, were extended to individuals in September 1990. These run twice daily departing from visitors' terrace Gate 33. Terminal 2 also has a good viewing gallery, but this is behind tinted glass.

Operators: Adria Airways (DC-9), Aeroflot (IL-62/86), Aerolineas Argentinas (Boeing 747), Aero Lloyd (DC-9, MD80), AeroMexico (Boeing 767), Aer Lingus (Boeing 737), Air Algerie (Boeing 727/737), Air Canada (Boeing 747/767), Air France (Airbus A320, Canadair Regional Jet, ATR-42), Air India (Boeing 747), Air Lanka (TriStar), Air Malta (Boeing 737, Airbus A320), Air Mauritius (Boeing 767), Air Moldova (Tu-134), Air Namibia (Boeing 747), Air New Zealand (Boeing 747), Air Portugal (Boeing 737, TriStar), Air Seychelles (Boeing 767), Air UK (BAe 146, Fokker 100), Air Zimbabwe (Boeing 767), Alitalia (DC-9, MD80), All Nippon (Boeing 747), American Airlines (Boeing 767), Austrian Airlines (MD80), Avianca (Boeing 747), Balkan (Airbus A320, Boeing 737), Baltic International (DC-9), Bangladesh Biman (DC-10), Belavia (Tu-134/154), British Airways (Boeing 737/757/767), Dash Eight), British Midland (Boeing 737, DC-9), Business Air (BAe 146), BWIA International (TriStar), Canadian Airlines (DC-10, Boeing 747), Cathay Pacific (Boeing 747), Condor (Boeing 737/757/747/767), Continental Airlines (Boeing 747, DC-10), Crossair (SAAB SF340), CSA Czechoslovak Airlines (Tu-134/154, ATR-72, Boeing 737, IL-62), Cyprus Airways (Airbus A310/320), Delta Air Lines (Airbus A310, Boeing 727/767, TriStar, MD11), Deutsche BA (Fokker 100), Estonian Air (Tu-134), EgyptAir (Airbus A320, Boeing 737/767), El Al (Boeing 747/757), Emirates (Airbus A310), Ethiopean Airlines (Boeing 757/767), Eurowings (ATR-42), Finnair (MD80), Garuda (MD11, Boeing 747), Germania (Boeing 737), Gulf Air (Boeing 767), Hapag-Lloyd (Airbus A310, Boeing 737), Iberia (Airbus A320, MD80), Icelandair (Boeing 737/757), Iran Air (Boeing 747), Istanbul Airlines (Boeing 727/737), Japan Airlines (Boeing 747), Kenya Airways (Airbus A310), KLM (Boeing 737, Fokker 100), Korean Air (Boeing 747), Kuwait Airways (Airbus A310, Boeing 747), LAN Chile (Boeing 767), Lithuanian Airlines (Yak-42), LOT Polish Airlines (ATR-72, Boeing 737), LTE (Boeing 757), LTU (Boeing 757/767, TriStar, MD11), Lufthansa (Airbus A300/310/320/321/340, Boeing 737/757, Dash Eight), Luxair (Fokker 50), Maersk Air (Fokker 50), Malaysian Airlines (Boeing 747), Malev (Boeing 737, Tu-134), Meridiana (DC-9, BAe 146), Middle East Airlines (Airbus A310, Boeing 707), Northwest Airlines (DC-10), Olympic Airways (Airbus A300, Boeing 737), Pakistan International (Airbus A310, Boeing 747), Philippine Airlines (Boeing 747), Qantas (Boeing 747), Royal Air Maroc (Boeing 737), Royal Brunei Airlines (Boeing 767), Royal Jordanian (Airbus A320, TriStar), Royal Nepal Airlines (Airbus A310), SABENA (Boeing 737), SAS (DC-9, MD80), Saudia (TriStar), Saxonia Airlines (Metro), Singapore Airlines (Boeing 747), South African Airways (Boeing 747), Spanair (MD80, Boeing 767), Sudan Airways (Airbus A310), Swissair (MD80, Fokker 100), Syrian Arab (Boeing 727/747), TACV Cabo Verde (Airbus A310), Tarom (Boeing 737, One-Eleven), Thai Airways International (Boeing 747), Tunis Air (Airbus A320, Boeing 727/737), Turkish Airlines (Airbus A310), Trans World (TriStar, Boeing 767), Tyrolean Airways (Dash Eight), Ukraine International (Boeing 737), United Airlines (Boeing 747/767), USAir (Boeing 767), Varig (Boeing 747/767, MD11), Viasa (DC-10), Viva Air (Boeing 737), Yemenia (Boeing 727),

Movements (1993): Total 352,100. Total passengers 31,945,000.

Runways: 07L/25R (13,123ft/4,000m), 07R/25L (13,123ft/4,000m), 18/36 (13,123ft/4,000m).

Radio frequencies: 119.9MHz, 124.85MHz (Tower), 120.8MHz (Approach), 120.15MHz (Departures), 121.8MHz (Ground).

Telephone: 069 690-1 (main switchboard) 069-690-3051 (information)

Operated by: Flughafen Frankfurt Main AG

Geneva (Cointrin)

Secondly only to Zürich in terms of traffic handled by the Swiss airports, Geneva began life in 1920 when a grass strip and wooden buildings were sufficient to cater for the scheduled services, the first being a link with Paris. These arrangements in fact sufficed until after the war, a period when the Swiss took the opportunity to lay a concrete runway in readiness for the predicted postwar boom in air transport.

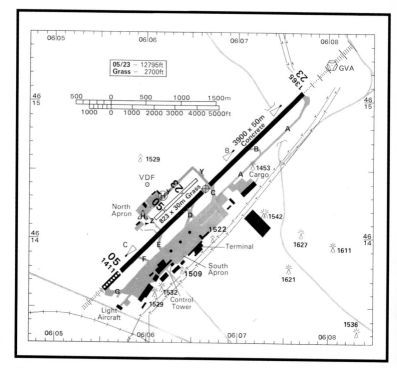

Together with a more substantial terminal, these facilities then served until well into the 1960s, but with the advent of much larger types, the Geneva Canton authorities took the decision to undertake a complete modernisation programme before the airport was overtaken by an embarrassing influx of passengers.

It was a very advanced scheme for its time, making use of three satellite buildings linked to the main terminal by underground tunnels. By this method the apron is not filled with buses or passengers walking to the aircraft. Instead the machines park radially around the satellites which contain a number of holding lounges for waiting travellers. All the normal formalities are carried out in the main building which also contains a departure lounge, but the majority of people prefer to proceed to the satellite immediately. This brings an added bonus for the authorities since the congestion is then kept to a minimum. Because of the restricted area of land available for expansion, an exchange of territory was agreed with France in 1956 so

that the runway could be extended towards the northeast. To simplify matters a 'French sector' was established within the terminal on the departures side, this being linked to a customs road leading directly into France at Fernay-Voltaire. Even by the early 1980s the Swiss had drawn up a plan which was entitled Horizon 2000. A major terminal will introduce two Y-shaped piers at either end of the main building to be reached by the rapid transit system similar to that employed between Gatwick North and South. From June 1987 access to the airport was greatly improved by the opening of the direct rail link making the airport station the terminus of the Lausanne-Geneva line. General aviation is handled on the far side of the runway although facilities exist for executive types beyond the cargo centre to the south of the terminal. Balair CTA's hangar and administration offices are also situated in this area.

Location and access: Situated 2.5 miles (4km) north of the city centre. Ample car parks are available and the Lausanne-

Chamonix-Lyon motorway passes alongside the airport with access points provided. TPG trolleybus route 10 runs from the city centre (Bel-Air and Cornivon station) every 12min with a journey time of 20min. Every 15min an SBB train leaves the airport station for Geneva-Cornevin taking 6min for the trip.

Terminal: A whole range of shops is situated in the departures hall embracing a wide range of goods with everything on sale that is normally associated with the country. Unfortunately, the cost is prohibitive. A number of restaurants and buffets are to be found, but these too are extremely expensive.

Spectator facilities: An excellent open first-floor terrace extends along much of the apron with access from alongside the restaurant building. There is a charge of SFr1 with entrance via a security check. It should be borne in mind that there are no toilets provided, so arrangements should be made accordingly. Opening times are between 09.00hrs and 19.00hrs, but occasionally the facility is closed when some high-ranking politician chooses the city as a suitable place for a chat with counterparts from other nations. From this admirable vantage point all movements can be seen and most photographed with ease. Geneva is an example of an airport that recognises the popularity of the public area and therefore has retained it by introducing a security check point at the entrance. By way of a change a saunter along to the holding point of runway 05 is worthwhile because although there is the usual fence, it contains a series of convenient holes. If this is not enough, then a nearby grassy bank gives a higher elevation. This location also overlooks the Aeroleasing apron; a company which specialises in long range airtaxi work. Airport tours are arranged but these are for groups of at least 15 persons. For bookings telephone the authority on 022-981122.

Operators: Adria Airways (DC-9), Aeroflot (IL-62/86), Aerolineas Argentinas (Boeing 747), Aero Lloyd (DC-9, MD80), AeroMexico (Boeing 767), Aer Lingus (Boeing 737), Air Algerie (Boeing 727/737), Air Canada (Boeing 747/767), Air France (Airbus A320, Canadair Regional Jet, ATR-42), Air India (Boeing 747), Air Lanka (TriStar), Air Malta (Boeing 737, Airbus A320), Air Mauritius (Boeing 767), Air Moldova (Tu-134), Air Namibia (Boeing 747), Air New Zealand (Boeing 747), Air Portugal (Boeing 737, TriStar), Air Seychelles (Boeing 767), Air UK (BAe 146, Fokker 100), Air Ukraine International (Boeing 737), Air Zimbabwe (Boeing 767), Alitalia (DC-9, MD80), All Nippon (Boeing 747), American Airlines (Boeing 767), Austrian Airlines (MD80), Avianca (Boeing 747), Balkan (Airbus A320, Boeing 737), Baltic International (DC-9), Bangladesh Biman (DC-10), Belavia (Tu-134/154), British Airways (Boeing 737/757/767, Dash Eight), British Midland (Boeing 737, DC-9), Business Air (BAe 146), BWIA International (TriStar), Canadian Airlines (DC-10, Boeing 747), Cathay Pacific (Boeing 747), Condor (Boeing 737/757/747/767), Continental Airlines (Boeing 747, DC-10), Crossair (SAAB SF340), CSA Czechoslovak Airlines (Tu-134/154, ATR-72, Boeing 737, IL-62), Cyprus Airways (Airbus A310/320), Delta Air Lines (Airbus A310, Boeing 727/767), TriStar, MD11), Deutsche BA (Fokker 100), Estonian Air (Tu-134), EgyptAir (Airbus A320, Boeing 737/767), El Al (Boeing 747/757), Emirates (Airbus A310), Ethiopian Airlines (Boeing 757/767), Eurowings (ATR-42), Finnair (MD80), Garuda (MD11, Boeing 747), Germania (Boeing 737), Gulf Air (Boeing 767), Hapag-Lloyd (Airbus A310, Boeing 737), Iberia (Airbus A320, MD80), Icelandair (Boeing 737/757), Iran Air (Boeing 747), Istanbul Airlines (Boeing 727/737), Japan Airlines (Boeing 747), Kenya Airways (Airbus A310), KLM (Boeing 737, Fokker 100), Korean Air (Boeing 747), Kuwait Airways (Airbus A310, Boeing 747), LAN Chile (Boeing 767), Lithuanian Airlines (Yak-42), LOT Polish Airlines (ATR-72, Boeing 737), LTE (Boeing 757), LTU (Boeing 757/767, TriStar, MD11), Lufthansa

Left:
Air Littoral uses ATR42s for its French services to Geneva.
A. S. Wright

(Airbus A300/310/320/321/340, Boeing 737/757, Dash Eight), Luxair (Fokker 50), Maersk Air (Fokker 50), Malaysian Airlines (Boeing 747), Malev (Boeing 737, Tu-134), Meridiana (DC-9, BAe 146), Middle East Airlines (Airbus A310, Boeing 707), Northwest Airlines (DC-10), Olympic Airways (Airbus A300, Boeing 737), Pakistan International (Airbus A310, Boeing 747), Philippine Airlines (Boeing 747), Qantas (Boeing 747), Royal Air Maroc (Boeing 737), Royal Brunei Airlines (Boeing 767), Royal Jordanian (Airbus A320, TriStar), Royal Nepal Airlines (Airbus A310), SABENA (Boeing 737), SAS (DC-9. MD80), Saudia (TriStar), Saxonia Airlines (Metro), Singapore Airlines (Boeing 747), South African Airways (Boeing 747), Spanair (MD80, Boeing 747), Sudan Airways (Airbus A310), Swissair (MD80, Fokker 100), Syrian Arab (Boeing 727/747), Boeing 747, (Airbus A321MD11),

Tarom (Boeing 737, One-Eleven), Thai Airways International (Boeing 747), Tunis Air (Airbus A320, Boeing 727/737), Turkish Airlines (Airbus A310), Trans World (TriStar, Boeing 767), Tyrolean Airways (Dash Eight), United Airlines (Boeing 747/767), USAir (Boeing 767), Varig (Boeing 747/767, MD11), Viasa (DC-10), Viva Air (Boeing 737), Yemenia (Boeing 727),

Movements (1993): Total 352,100. Total passengers 31,945,000.

Runways: 05/23 (12,795ft/3,900m), 05/23 (2,700ft/823m — grass).

Radio frequencies: 118.7MHz, 119.7MHz, 119.9MHz (Tower/Approach), 121.9MHz (Ground).

Telephone: (22) 717 71 11

Operated by: Department of Public Economy of the State of Geneva

Helsinki (Vantaa)

When air transport was introduced in Finland, a city centre seaplane base was established at Katajanokka. Although convenient, this type of aircraft was very limited in scope so in 1938 a more conventional landplane airport was provided at Malmi. This continued in service until the present complex at Vantaa was officially opened on 26 October 1952, although it had been used during the course of that summer's Olympic Games. Nevertheless another 17 years passed before a permanent terminal was completed, a temporary wooden structure serving during the lengthy wait. At least the time was spent usefully by the planners because after 1969 no further work was necessary until the building was extended between 1980 and 1983. Vantaa's first runway was only 6,562ft (2,000m) long, but by 1956 a second had been constructed, both subsequently extended several times until the main strip now stretches for 11,286ft (3,440m). Although much superior to its predecessor, Vantaa's position was dictated by the need to accommodate jet-age aircraft, so inevitably it is further from the city.

Weather conditions in these northern latitudes are frequently inhospitable, but the Finns are suitably equipped to handle vast deposits of snow and ice. Accordingly the airport possesses a large fleet of vehicles dedicated to keeping it open at all times with hardly a break in traffic. Needless to say, this is a full-time occupation during the long winter months.

Vantaa has been Finnair's main base since 1952, joined in due course by most of the country's other aviation companies, such as Karair and Finnaviation.

In addition to the third runway to be provided in the latter half of the 1990s, several other major developments have already taken place at the airport during the decade. Work began in early 1991 on the construction of a new domestic terminal which was completed in early 1992. At this point the existing premises were refurbished and began handling only international traffic. In association with this expansion a new multi-storey car park has been opened, while the surface areas have been considerably increased in size.

Location and access: Situated 12 miles (19.3km) north of the city centre near to the Tuusula motorway. Charges vary in the car parks depending on whether short term, 48hr, long term, open air or under cover. Finnair buses operate from Helsinki's city air terminal to the airport at about 20 to 30min intervals depending on the time of day. Sirolan Liikenne route 615 also links Vantaa with the Central railway station, the journey taking between 30 and 35min.

Terminal: This contains four restaurants, two bars and three buffets. There are several shops and other services both in the transit hall and unrestricted areas. Although airbridges are used for loading, these all project from the main building rather than from piers.

Spectator facilities: A balcony originally provided for visitors' use has been closed

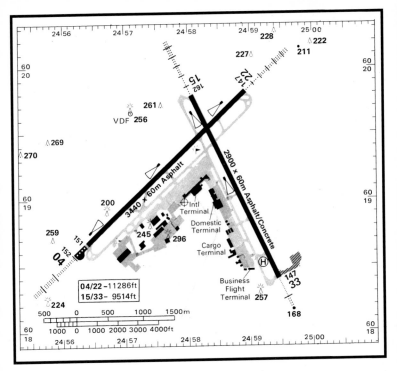

for security reasons, but the Fly-Inn restaurant in the International terminal provides good views of most movements. From this vantage point photography is possible through the glass with care. Alternatively, if Runway 15/33 is in use then the adjacent car park 11 can provide a reasonable spot, albeit sometimes chilly. Finland's aviation museum is located at the airport and can be reached after a 15min walk. It contains various vintage types plus other items and photographs relevant to the country's history.

Operators: Aeroflot (Tu-134/154), Air Botnia (Bandeirante, Jetstream 31), Air China (Boeing 747), Air Europa (Boeing 737/757), Air France (Boeing 737), Austrian Airlines (MD80), Balkan (Tu-154), British Airways (Boeing 737/757), Channel Express (Electra), CSA Czechoslovak Airlines (Boeing 737, IL-62), Delta Air Lines (Airbus A310, TriStar), El Al (Boeing 757), Estonian Air (Tu-134, Yak-40), Finnair (DC-9/10, MD80/11, Airbus A300), Finnaviation (SAAB SF340), Iberia (MD80), Kar-Air (ATR-72),

KLM (Boeing 737), Latavio Latvian Airlines (An-24), Lauda Air (Canadair Regional Jet), Lietuva (Yak-40), LOT Polish Airlines (Boeing 737), Lufthansa (Boeing 737, Canadair Regional Jet), Malev (Boeing 737, Tu-154), Pegasus (Boeing 737), Premiair (Airbus A320), SABENA (Boeing 737), SAS (DC-9, MD80), Sterling European (Boeing 727), Swissair (MD80), TNT (BAe 146), Transavia (Boeing 737/757), Transwede (MD80).

Movements (1993): Total 105,600. Total passengers 6,133,000.

Runways: 04/22 (11,286ft/3,440m), 15/33 (9,514ft/2,900m). A third is planned for the late 1990s.

Radio frequencies: 118.6MHz, 119.7MHz (Tower), 119.1MHz (Approach), 129.85MHz (Radar), 121.8MHz (Ground).

Telephone: (0) 82771

Operated by: Helsinki Airport Authority

London (Gatwick)

Officially the site became an airport on 6 June 1936 when it was formally declared open for commercial flying by the Secretary of State for Air. Six years earlier, in August 1930, flying at Gatwick had begun to be very popular with the horse racing fraternity due to its close proximity to the course. When the airfield was earmarked for development the planners incorporated several novel features in the design including an underground passageway to the adjacent railway station and the provision of a circular terminal building with covered walkways to the parked aircraft. Although several operators moved into the newly created facility, unfortunately Gatwick suffered from waterlogging from time to time, causing some to forsake their new home.

A military presence began in 1937 when the Tiger Moths and Harts of No 19 E&RFTS took up residence, which speeded the provision of additional buildings. This training establishment was closed at the outbreak of war, an event which also decreed that civil flying was suspended for the duration. Initially RAF Blenheims became the occupants, but in September 1940 the station came under the control of Army Co-Operation Command. Thereafter Lysanders and Tomahawks became a familiar sight until replaced with Mustangs in 1942, this type taking part in the Dieppe operation in August. In the middle of the following year Gatwick became part of No 11 Group so the local scene was thereafter dominated by Spitfires as various squadrons spent short periods at the airfield. Most of the operational activity involved escort duties or sweeps along the Channel, an occupation which continued until after D-Day in 1944. In the run-up to the invasion of France, Gatwick had also become the base for photo-reconnaissance Mustang units charged with the task of providing up-to-date information on the disposition of the German forces. By August the war had moved on, leaving the airfield with only non-operational activities for the remainder of its

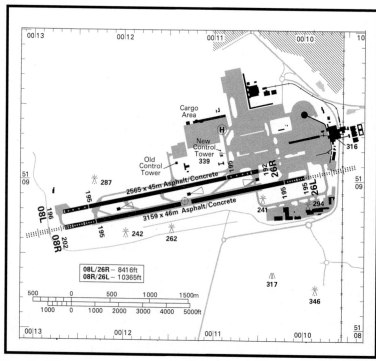

military career. Two years later the RAF relinquished its control, which passed to the Ministry of Civil Aviation.

Even at that early stage some thought was given to the possibility of Gatwick becoming a London airport, but it was by no means certain that another would be necessary to assist Heathrow. By 1952 there were no doubts left; Gatwick would be needed. When the plans were finalised the area selected was positioned to the north of the original site, the proposed single runway stretching for 7,000ft/2,133m towards the west. Access to the railway was still possible, although a new station was required near to the box-like terminal building. It was on 9 June 1958 that the opening ceremony was performed by HM The Queen and HRH Prince Philip, a Heron of the Royal Flight bringing the distinguished visitors to the scene.

For several years the new airport was able to cope with its traffic, much of which was provided by the charter carriers, but with the creation of British United Airways in 1960 the volume was considerably increased. Not far away, Heathrow was also feeling the strain, so it was decided to implement an expansion programme to relieve both airports. Gatwick's terminal was effectively doubled in size and the runway lengthened to 8,200ft/2,500m, but with the provision of a third London airport abandoned in the early 1970s, yet another even more ambitious development scheme was begun. Again a vast terminal expansion was involved including the addition of a satellite connected to the main building by a rapid transit system. Access was further improved by a direct link with the M23 motorway, while British Rail's train services became both frequent and fast. Airside changes included additional parking areas and taxiways, while an emergency runway was laid parallel to the existing strip with completion in October 1985. Ideally Gatwick would benefit from its regular use to facilitate simultaneous landings and take-offs, but unfortunately the separation distance does not comply with the safety limits. By this time the main runway had been extended once again, this time taking it to 10,363ft/3,159m in length.

After the removal of most charter flights from Heathrow, Gatwick became the main terminal for such operations in the London area, although scheduled movements also steadily increased as more and more airlines opened up services. Both British Caledonian and Dan-Air contributed considerably to the growth, but the advent of transatlantic flights by wide-bodied types was largely responsible for the need for yet more terminal space. It was not possible to provide this around the original building, so a second complex was planned on the north side which was duly opened for business in March 1988. All British Airways flights were transferred to the new facility, to be joined gradually by other refugees from the South Terminal.

In the 1980s Air Europe became a major force at Gatwick as its involvement in scheduled services became greater. Together with its IT work, the airline accounted for some 10% of the traffic at the airport, so when the company collapsed in March 1991 it had a marked effect on the traffic figures. Fortunately it was only temporary because there were more than enough eager carriers willing to take over the commitments. The decision to give newcomers the opportunity to have access to Heathrow was responsible for a number of moves from Gatwick, but the void was soon filled by others keen to serve London whichever gateway was allocated. The growing shortage of runway space in the southeast of England was responsible for a survey into the various options available, but it seems very unlikely that a second strip will now be laid at Gatwick.

The first phase of an £80 million redevelopment programme was opened in the spring of 1994. This produced a remodelled North Terminal international departure lounge complete with a large balcony giving views over the airport. Later in the summer, a three-storey pavilion was completed, housing first and business class lounges. The terminal is now equipped with three additional stands for BA European flights. South Terminal is also included in the redevelopment plans, with an extension to the international departure lounge to provide a balcony floor, plus more shops and restaurants. Improvements to the check-in concourse will result in a more spacious environment for this busy area and is due for completion in 1995.

Location and access: Situated 28 miles (45km) south of London with a direct link to the M23 motorway at Junction 9. Short-term multi-storey car parking with open long-term, both with graduated charges. The multi-storey car parks should be used only for stays of under 8hrs. If an extended stay is contemplated it is more economic to use public transport. By rail the Gatwick

Express runs nonstop between London Victoria station and the airport's South Terminal every 15min during the day, taking 30min for the journey. During the night the trains are hourly and take up to 15min longer to complete the trip. An alternative Thameslink service runs half-hourly from Kings Cross, Blackfriars and London Bridge taking some 35min for the trip from the latter. There is a direct transit link from Gatwick station to the North Terminal. Speedlink coaches connect Gatwick with Heathrow every 20min, each sortie scheduled to take 60min, but this depends on the road conditions on the M25 motorway. Route 777 runs to Victoria coach station while the Jetlink 747 visit Heathrow, Luton and Stansted airports. Local services C1, C2, 405 & 422 operate to both Crawley and Horley. There is a bus information desk in the international arrivals hall at Gatwick (Tel: 01293 502116 south and 01293 502320 north).

Terminals: Both main terminals contain restaurants and snack bars. Shops and banks are also much in evidence.

Spectator facilities: A gallery situated on the roof of the South Terminal building gives good views of all movements although some are rather distant. There is an admission charge and opening hours vary according to the season. A refreshment buffet is a welcome facility available, while the provision of TV monitors for checking arrivals and departures is very valuable. As a photographic vantage point the terrace has its limitations, although shots are possible of some of the aircraft using the satellite and the nearer centre pier stands. The building extension under way in 1994 has restricted the scope still further, but the terrace remains a reasonable viewing area. Unfortunately, many of the more interesting charter types are often banished to the far stands beyond the piers.

Operators: Aigle Azur (Bandeirante), Air Afrique (Airbus A310), Air Club International (Boeing 747), Air Columbus (Boeing 737), Air Europa (Boeing 737/757), Air France (Boeing 737, Fellowship), Air Jet (BAe 146), Air Liberte (MD80), Air Liberte Tunisie (MD80), Air Malta (Airbus A320, Boeing 737, Avro RJ70), Air New Zealand (Boeing 747), Air Ops (TriStar), Air Portugal (Boeing 737, TriStar), Air Seychelles (Boeing 767), Airtours (MD80, Airbus A320, Boeing

Above: The satellite stands also offer opportunities for photographs at Gatwick. Virgin's 747-400 G-VFAB became the subject for this illustration. *AJW*

Oposite Right: Meridiana DC-9-51 I-SMEJ moves on to its Gatwick stand, but this shot is now more difficult to achieve due to building work. *AJW*

757/767), Air Transat (TriStar), Air UK (BAe 146, Fokker 100), Air UK Leisure (Boeing 737), Airworld (Airbus A320), Air Zimbabwe (Boeing 767), Air 2000 (Boeing 757, Airbus A320), Alitalia (DC-9, MD80), American Airlines (Boeing 767, MD11), American Trans Air (TriStar, Boeing 757), Arkia (Boeing 757), Austrian Airlines (MD80), Balair CTA (MD80), Balkan (Tu-154), Baltic International (Boeing 727, Tu-134), BASE Regional (Jetstream, SAAB SF340), Braathens (Boeing 737), Britannia Airways (Boeing 757/767), British Airways (Boeing 737/747/767, DC-10), Brit Air (ATR-42, SAAB SF340), British Mediterranean (Airbus A320), British World (One-Eleven), Caledonian Airways (Airbus A320, Boeing 757, TriStar, DC-10), Canada 3000 (Boeing 757), Centennial (MD80), CityFlyer Express (ATR-42/72, Short SD3-60), Continental Airlines (DC-10, Boeing 747), Cyprus Airways (Airbus A310), Delta Air Lines (Airbus A310, Boeing 767, TriStar), El Al (Boeing 757), Emirates (Airbus A300), Eurofly (DC-9), European Airlines (Airbus A300), Eurowings (ATR-42/72), Excalibur Airways (Airbus A320), Futura (Boeing 737), Garuda (Boeing 747, MD11), GB Airways (Boeing 737), Gill Air (Short SD3-60, ATR-42), Istanbul Airlines (Boeing 727/737), Jersey European (Friendship, BAe 146), Lauda Air (Boeing 737/767), Leisure International (Boeing 767), Lithuanian Airlines (Boeing 737), Maersk Air (Boeing 737), Meridiana (DC-9, MD80, BAe 146), Monarch Airlines (Boeing 757, Airbus A300/320), Northwest Airlines (Boeing 747), Oasis (MD80), Onur Air (Airbus A320), Palair Macedonia (Fokker 100), Palmair Flightline (BAe 146), Pegasus (Boeing 737), Philippine Airlines (Boeing 747), Qatar Airways (Airbus A310), Regional Airlines (SAAB SF340, Jetstream 31), Royal Airlines (TriStar), Royal Bahamas (DC-10), Royal Jordanian (Airbus A310), Royal Nepal Airlines (Airbus A310), Royal Air Maroc (Boeing 737), Ryanair (Boeing 737), Sabre Airways (Boeing 727, 737), Spanair (MD80), Tarom (One-Eleven, Boeing 737), TAT European (Fokker 100, Fellowship), Transavia (Boeing 737), Transwede (Fokker 100), Trans World (Boeing 747/767), Ukraine International (Boeing 737), Virgin Atlantic (Airbus A320/340, Boeing 747), Viva Air (Boeing 737), Yemenia (Boeing 727).

Movements (1993): Total 174.700. Total passengers 20,065,000.

Runways: 08R/26L (10,364ft/3,159m), 08L/26R (8,415ft/2,565m) — used only in emergencies or if 08R/26L is closed; otherwise it serves as a taxiway.

Radio frequencies: 124.225MHz (Tower), 118.95MHz, 126.825MHz (Approach).

Telephone: (01293) 535353.

Operated by: Gatwick Airport Ltd.

London (Heathrow)

Since its opening in 1946, Heathrow has become one of the world's leading international airports with over 70 airlines providing services to all parts of the world. Almost all of the movements are those of scheduled traffic with very few charters permitted, although executive aircraft are regular visitors and the cargo facility opened in 1968 continues to handle a considerable amount of business. Compared with some of its European counterparts, Heathrow presents a jumble of buildings of varying designs all packed into the restricted space available in the central area. Even the much acclaimed Terminal 4 does little to redress the balance. Nevertheless the airports on the continent do not have to contend with the same volume of traffic as London, so the emphasis has always had to be on the speedy movement of passengers rather than elegance. Much of the blame for the problem stems from its early days when it was planned as a standard RAF airfield with a triangular runway pattern. Even when this was quickly abandoned the choice of layout still favoured the centre island arrangement. Breaking away from this was the only solution when a new terminal was urgently needed at the end of the 1970s. Its opening in April 1986 certainly brought some relief because at that stage all of British Airways' intercontinental services, together with the airline's Paris, Amsterdam and Athens flights, were all transferred from either Terminal 1 or 3. Also accommodated in the new Terminal 4 are KLM, Air Malta and Air Lanka.

A long-standing policy was changed in 1991 when the authorities agreed to allow new carriers access to Heathrow. This relaxation of the rules came after American Airlines and United Airlines bought transatlantic routes from TWA and Pan Am respectively. A number of companies subsequently transferred their operations from Gatwick in the belief that travellers would prefer using London's premier airport. Charter operators were also allowed back after an absence of over 20 years, with several tour companies offering Heathrow as an alternative departure point in their summer programmes. Needless to say, this influx did nothing to improve the congestion both land and airside, so investigations began into the feasibility of a fifth terminal and another runway to the north of the Bath Road. The latter proposal revives the scheme originally planned for Heathrow in the 1940s, but abandoned as unnecessary at the time.

Location and access: Situated 14 miles (22.5km) west of central London with access direct from the M4 motorway at Junction 4 or the A4 to the central area. Terminal 4 is alongside the A30 and can be reached from the M25. Each of the four terminals has its own short-term car park with rapidly escalating charges after the first two hours. One long-term car park serving all terminals is located on the eastern boundary. A courtesy bus shuttles backwards and forwards at frequent intervals. If a stay is likely to exceed two hours it is more sensible to use this park. Bearing in mind the amount of public transport on offer, it is often cheaper to leave the car outside the airport and catch a bus or train. By using the Piccadilly Line from central London it is possible to make the journey in 47min. Trains stop at Hatton Cross on the boundary of the airport before travelling in a clockwise direction to Terminal 4 and Heathrow Central. The return to London takes the train around the remainder of the loop to Hatton Cross once again. Numerous local buses call at the central bus station, while coaches to most parts of the country leave either from Heathrow or via a direct link with Victoria coach station. Express services are operated on this route by Green Line's Fleetline 767 and London Transport's Airbus which also visits Euston railway station in its travels. A direct Speedlink coach links Heathrow with Gatwick and Stansted at regular intervals, while Jetlink 747 has a similar purpose but includes Luton in its itinerary. As an alternative, Rail/Air links are available with coaches ferrying passengers to and from Woking and Reading BR stations for onward travel by InterCity or local trains to the west. At the moment BR is building a line to the airport so that fast trains can be operated in a similar manner to those serving Gatwick.

Terminals: All four have lounge areas, shops, restaurants, bars, buffets, bank and post offices. Terminal 4 has fewer facilities in the public area. Terminal 1 handles all British Airways' (European Division) flights (except Paris, Amsterdam and Athens) plus all other UK airlines as well as Aer Lingus. As a result, congestion is not unknown in the building, particularly around the arrivals area. A major improvement scheme to enlarge the facilities on the northern side of Terminal 1 has provided more gate-lounges

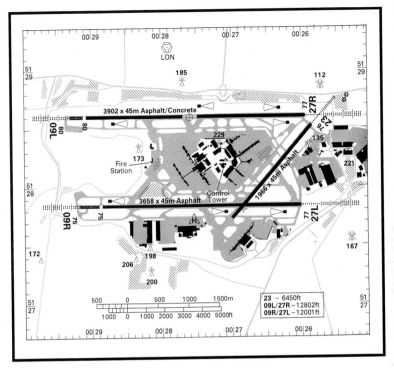

and airbridge-equipped stands. Following the opening of Terminal 4 several other carriers using the centre complex were relocated in order to achieve a better distribution of traffic in the terminals. As a result, Cyprus Airways, El Al, Finnair, Onur Air, SABENA and South African Airways are handled by Terminal 1. The remaining European airlines use Terminal 2 with the exception of Icelandair, Lithuanian Airlines, SAS and Virgin, which are allocated to Terminal 3.

Spectator facilities: A large roof terrace is provided over Terminal 2. It has its own snackbar and is open daily from 10.00hrs until dusk. There is an admission charge. It is a fine vantage point for viewing purposes, all movements being visible if somewhat distant at times. Unfortunately, through the years the photographic opportunities have steadily declined, mainly due to the number of new buildings that have grown along the front of the terminal. However, while it is now difficult to obtain reasonable ground shots of even BA aircraft, with luck it is not

impossible. Without doubt, a trip to Schiphol, Düsseldorf or Frankfurt is far more rewarding and less frustrating. An alternative viewing facility is being considered by the BAA.

Operators: Adria Airways (MD80), Aer Lingus (Boeing 737), Aeroflot (Airbus A310, IL-86, Tu-154), Aerolineas Argentinas (Boeing 747), Air Algerie (Boeing 727), Air Canada (Boeing 747/767), Air China (Boeing 747), Air France (Airbus A300/320, Boeing 737), Air India (Boeing 747), Air Lanka (TriStar), Air Malta (Boeing 737, Airbus A320), Air Mauritius (Boeing 747), Air Namibia (Boeing 747), Air Portugal (Airbus A320, Boeing 737), Air UK (Friendship), Alitalia (MD80, Airbus A300/321), All Nippon (Boeing 747), American Airlines (MD11, Boeing 767), Ariana Afghan (Boeing 727), Austrian Airlines (MD80), Balkan (Airbus A320), Bangladesh Biman (DC-10), British Airways (Airbus A320, Boeing 737/747/757/767, Fellowship, Concorde), British Midland (Boeing 737, DC-9, Fokker 100, Jetstream), Brymon Airways (Dash

Seven/Eight), BWIA International (TriStar), Canadian Airlines (Boeing 767, DC-10), Cathay Pacific (Boeing 747, Airbus A340), Croatia Airlines (Boeing 737), Crossair (Avro RJ85, BAe 146), CSA Czechoslovak Airlines (Boeing 737), Cyprus Airways (Airbus A310), EgyptAir (Airbus A300/320), El Al (Boeing 747/757), Emirates (Airbus A310), Ethiopian Airlines (Boeing 757/767), EVA Air (Boeing 747), Finnair (MD80, DC-9), Garuda (Boeing 747), Gulf Air (Airbus A340, Boeing 767), Iberia (Airbus A320, MD80, Boeing 757), Icelandair (Boeing 757), Iran Air (Boeing 747), Istanbul Airlines (Boeing 727), Japan Airlines (Boeing 747), Kenya Airways (Airbus A310), KLM (Fokker 50, Boeing 737, Fellowship, Airbus A310), Korean Air (Boeing 747), Kuwait Airways (Airbus A300), Lithuanian Airlines (Yak-42), LOT Polish Airlines (Boeing 737), Lufthansa (Airbus A300/310/320/321, Boeing 737), Luxair (Boeing 737), Malaysian Airlines (Boeing 747), Malev (Tu-154), Manx Airlines (BAe 146, ATP), Middle East Airlines (Airbus A310, Boeing 747), Nigeria Airways (DC-10), Olympic Airways (Airbus A300), Onur Air (Airbus A320), Pakistan International (Boeing 747), Philippine Airlines (Boeing 747), Qantas (Boeing 747), Royal Air Maroc (Boeing 737), Royal Brunei (Boeing 767), Royal Jordanian (Airbus A310), SAS (MD80, DC-9, Boeing 767), SABENA (Dash Eight, Boeing 737), Saudia (Boeing 747), Singapore Airlines (Boeing 747), South African Airways (Boeing 747), Sudan Airways (Airbus A310), Swissair (MD80, Airbus A310), Tajik Air (Boeing 747), Tarom (Boeing 737), Thai International (Boeing 747), Turkish Airlines (Airbus A310, Boeing 737), United Airlines (Boeing 747/767), Uzbekistan Airways (IL-62), Varig (Boeing 747), Viasa (DC-10), Viva Air (Boeing 737).

Movements (1993): Total 394,100. Total passengers 47,602,000.

Runways: 09R/27L (12,000ft/3,658m), 09L/27R (12,802ft/3,902m), 05/23 (7,733ft/2,357m).

Radio frequencies: 118.50MHz, 118.70MHz, 124.475MHz (Tower), 119.725MHz, 134.975MHz, (Approach), 135.125MHz, 127.55MHz (Radar), 121.9MHz (Ground).

Telephone: (0181) 759 4321
Operated by: Heathrow Airport Ltd

Top:
Istanbul Airlines operates its Boeing 737-400s to Heathrow, with TC-AGA in service for this flight. *AJW*

Above:
Company-operated Boeing 727 VR-BKC and Petrolair's 757 HB-IEE at Heathrow's Terminal 3. *AJW*

Luxembourg (Findel)

Although a number of fields in Luxembourg were used by light aircraft from the earliest days of flying, it was 1937 before a serious attempt was made to attract commercial services to the country. In March the government announced its intention to build a new airport at Findel, some three miles from the capital. World War 2 intervened before the site was completed, although the Americans provided some temporary buildings during their presence in 1945. Two years later the runway was completely relaid

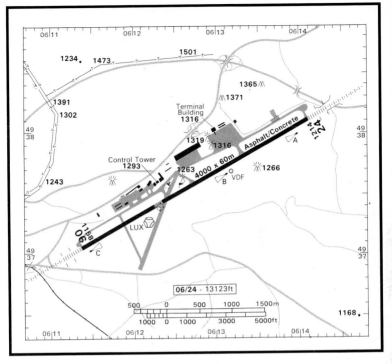

and extended to 3,805ft, sufficient to allow the safe operation of DC-3s and the like. Further works in 1948 took the strip to 4,921ft with land earmarked to add another 1,600ft in the future. At the same time a brand-new terminal was constructed to handle the modest flow of passengers, while nearby a hangar large enough to accommodate four DC-3s was provided.

When fully operational, Findel received 679 foreign aircraft during 1947, of which 90% were DC-3s. Many of the movements were originated by Sabena, which inaugurated a scheduled run to Basle using this type. On 10 January 1948 Luxembourg Airlines was formed, a company in which Scottish Aviation had a financial interest and provided technical support. A month or so later the carrier commenced operations on routes that linked its headquarters with Frankfurt, Paris and Zürich, but in 1950 the British company withdrew and all services were suspended for a time. With the assistance of Seaboard and Western Airlines operations were restarted, but finally

Luxembourg Airlines ceased trading in 1958.

In April 1962 a reorganised company known as Luxair resumed flying on the same three routes using a Fokker Friendship leased from the manufacturer. At this time the airport's capacity was not stretched, but with the emergence of the flag carrier it was not long before plans were announced for a new terminal, cargo centre and maintenance facility. Target date for completion of the complex was the end of 1975; in fact the terminal opened for business on 1 November of that year. In addition to the European flights offered by Luxair, Findel also became the departure point for low-cost transatlantic charters which staged through Iceland on their way to America. Subsequently Icelandair has developed scheduled services over similar routes using DC-8s and, more recently, Boeing 757s. A good deal of freight passes through the airport, much of it carried in the Boeing 747s of locally-based Cargolux. The company has now added two Srs 400 to its fleet and has subsequently carried a record load of over 116 tonnes direct from Seattle to Luxembourg. The type's long-range capability also allows Cargolux to fly direct from its base to Hong Kong with a payload of 97 tonnes. As a result of the steady increase in the volume of cargo handled by the airport, the construction of new facilities was started in January 1994, which when completed will provide adequate accommodation for the traffic of the next decade.

Location and access: Situated 3 miles (6km) northeast of the city off road N1. Luxembourg Community Transport bus route 9 links the central railway station with the airport at regular intervals, taking 22min for the journey. There is ample car parking space with charges dependent on duration of stay. Both Belgian and Luxembourg currency is accepted.

Terminal: The single three-storey building is still adequate for the volume of traffic handled, although there is a project to build three interconnected piers in the future. All the usual facilities such as buffet, shop and bank are included within.

Spectator facilities: A fine rooftop terrace is provided giving excellent views of all movements. It is also a very good vantage point for photography although the sun can present a problem in the afternoons. There is now no charge levied for entrance to the facility. If at any time it is closed there are terraces at either side of the terminal which can prove useful for some shots. For the patient there is the reward of some interesting subjects, but since movements are well spaced at times a visit is more profitable if organised after checking airline schedules. It is also possible to obtain some good views of freight aircraft on the Cargolux apron, including the regularly visiting Aeroflot IL-76s, African 707s and the 747F of China Airlines.

Operators: Aeroflot (IL-62/76, Tu-154), Air Belgium (Boeing 737), Air Portugal (Boeing 737), Balkan (Tu-154), British Airways (Airbus A320, Boeing 757), Cargolux (Boeing 747), Condor (Boeing 757), Crossair (SAAB SF340), Hapag-Lloyd (Boeing 737), Icelandair (Boeing 757), KLM CityHopper (SAAB SF340), Luxair (Boeing 737, Brasilia, Fokker 50), SABENA (Brasilia), SAS (Fokker 50), Sunline (Gulfstream 1), Transavia (Boeing 737) and Tunis Air (Boeing 727/737).

Movements (1993): Total 65,617 (scheduled 25,745/non-scheduled 6,674/general aviation 6,080). Total passengers 1,106,750.

Runway: 06/24 (13,123ft/4,000m).

Radio frequencies: 118.1MHz (Tower), 118.45MHz (Approach).

Telephone: 4798-2311/2315

Operated by: Administration de l'Aéroport

Manchester International

Manchester has been the UK's third busiest airport for many years, a position it is likely to retain. Package holiday flights in particular have contributed greatly to the impressive growth, attracting travellers from far and wide as the tour operators continued to offer a widening range of destinations for the sun-seekers. There has also been a significant increase in the variety of scheduled services on offer, including more transatlantic flights. Fifty years ago the generation of the day was either happy with the nearby coastal resorts of northern Britain or stayed at home. No one could possibly have envisaged the change in habits at the time of the airport's opening on 25 June 1938.

Then known as Ringway, Manchester airport had received its first commercial arrival on the previous day when a KLM DC-2 completed its trip from Amsterdam. Once everything had settled down, schedules began to build up, but it was not to last. With the outbreak of war the airport ended its brief association with civil aviation. Although not actually requisitioned by the Air Ministry, Manchester became the home of a number of military units, probably the best known being the Central Landing School from which emerged No 1 Parachute Training School. By the end of the war over 60,000 troops had passed through the gates to make over 500,000 jumps from Whitleys and Dakotas. In addition to this major activity, gliders were also in evidence until space forced a move to a less cramped locality. As if this were not enough, both Fairey and Avro flew their newly built products from the airfield and RAF operational squadrons used Ringway for a while when defending the city.

Postwar commercial services were resumed in 1946, the first schedule being an international link with Paris flown by Air France. KLM was also quick to reappear with its Amsterdam sector, but domestic

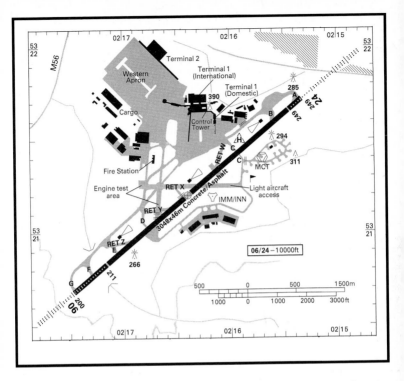

operations were limited in the UK at this time. This was mainly because of much uncertainty and discontent following the decision that the newly created British European Airways would operate all services. In the event it was unable to commence work on many of the internal routes in 1946 due to lack of resources, so most were contracted to the smaller companies as an interim measure. Although the main line sectors were taken over by the state airline in 1947, it was neither keen nor able to absorb the many seasonal links. Manchester therefore retained its connection with both Jersey and the Isle of Man, routes which produced such impressive load factors for the operator of the day that BEA decided that it was in its interest to take them over in future.

By the 1950s a new terminal had been built with all modern facilities, but despite the improvements there was still a reluctance by BOAC to introduce long-haul services from the airport. This omission was duly noted by the Belgian flag carrier,

Sabena, resulting in the start of a new schedule to New York. BOAC was at last forced to move its northern UK terminal to the growing Ringway, but it was not until 1954 that the first Stratocruiser departed for the American city, albeit via Prestwick. Meanwhile BEA had tended to ignore the potential of the European sectors, which had allowed airlines such as Aer Lingus and SAS to exercise their fifth freedom rights on routes passing through Manchester. Traffic growth had begun to outstrip the capacity of the airport by the late 1950s, so plans were initiated for a brand new terminal to be constructed to modern standards. When opened in 1962 two piers projected from the impressive main building across the extensive apron. Its arrival was not a moment too soon because for the first time over 1 million passengers were handled during that year. A significant impact was now being made by the inclusive tour flights, of which more and more were being offered by specialised airlines. At first these mainly linked Manchester with the

Above: The CSA Tu-134 OK-HFL turns off the runway in front of the spectators' viewing area at Manchester. *AJW*

Mediterranean coastal areas, but soon the more adventurous were taking advantage of the cheap transatlantic charters on offer.

With the arrival of the so-called jumbo era, a new international pier complete with airbridges was built at the western end of the terminal, a project which was completed in 1974. In conjunction with this expansion some major internal alterations were carried out in the main building. Any of the new generation airliners could now be accommodated with ease, so to put the finishing touch to the airport the name Ringway was finally replaced by the grander title of Manchester International.

Although traffic still increased each year, there remained a certain reticence on the part of the national carrier to become too involved in the northern airport. In 1981 it actually suspended all its transatlantic activities, at the same time severely trimming back both its European and domestic operations. Fortunately there were foreign airlines willing to introduce schedules, although not all found them to be a commercial success. Subsequently BA reintroduced many of its links with the continent, but it still has a very limited range of long-haul services on offer. Instead it prefers to ferry passengers to Heathrow on the shuttle to connect with flights elsewhere.

Further extensions to the airport included a satellite C pier area at the end of the international C pier, followed by the erection of a separate domestic terminal to replace the A pier previously employed. Costing £27 million, it was opened in the spring of 1989 and is completely self-contained, with its own restaurants, shops and multi-storey car park. There is a linkway with the main concourse for the benefit of transfer passengers.

While this development was intended to handle 2.5 million travellers annually, in the long term more substantial expansion was deemed necessary for the 1990s if the traffic continued to steadily increase. Therefore in 1988 plans were approved by the airport authority for the construction of a brand-new terminal located on the northwest side of the existing complex. Apart from that needed for the diversion of a local road, all of the land required was already owned by the airport.

An interesting design was chosen with a two-storey building fronting the much-enlarged apron. The main concourse is flanked on either side by long fingers along which the various airbridge-equipped gates are positioned. Provision was made for a remote island pier to be erected parallel to this structure at a later date, which will be reached via two underground passageways. Manchester International has now been given its own dedicated rail link with a station in the heart of the complex. When opened, the latest improvements to the airport were able to assist with the 12 million passengers using the facilities in 1993, a total forecast to rise to 20 million by the end of the decade. Plans are actively under way for the provision of a second runway, a scheme not accepted without objections from the local community.

Location and access: Situated 10 miles (16km) south of Manchester, directly connected to the M56 motorway at Junction 5. A large short-term multi-storey car park adjoins Terminal 1 and is charged per half hour, rising swiftly after the first period. The long-term park is more economic for stays over four hours or so, while the Southside Saver offers both covered and outside parking at a cheaper rate. A direct rail service operates every 15min between Piccadilly/Oxford Road stations to Terminal 1 with a journey time of between 17min and 22min. Bus links with Terminal 2 are provided. Airbus service 200 runs from the City Centre (Piccadilly) with a journey time of 25min. Services 100, 757 and 44 all link the city centre with the airport via different routes and varying journey times. Direct coach services are operated to a number of towns and cities in the north. Every two hours the National Express service 825 sets off for Heathrow and Gatwick, a destination reached in some 7hr.

Terminals: Now known as Terminal 1, the orginal building contains a restaurant, buffet and various shops. The adjoining domestic terminal contains a similar selection but on a smaller scale. Terminal 2 is also self-contained although courtesy buses are used to convey passengers to and from the rail station, unlike Terminal 1, which has a covered travelator link.

Spectator facilities: The one-time excellent roof terrace is now much reduced in size and offers limited views of the apron. These do not include the international Pier C stands, but the nearby multi-storey car park compensates. Fortunately, the airport authority recognised the considerable interest shown by visitors and the need to replace the lost facilities. It was decided to develop the site of an old brickworks on the southwest side of the runway into a viewing area with free car parking. This was duly completed together with a mound for the convenience of photographers. The result has proved very popular with enthusiasts and casual visitors alike. Preferably, Runway 06 needs to be in use, when some excellent landing shots can be obtained, but even without this bonus the vantage point is well worth visiting. To find the viewing area it is necessary to follow the airport perimeter with a series of right turns from the terminal, or off the A583 Wilmslow road. It is not particularly well signposted.

Operators: Adria Airways (DC-9), Aeroflot (Tu-154), Aer Lingus (Boeing 737, Fokker 50), Air Canada (Boeing 767), Air Club International (Boeing 747), (Air Europa (Boeing 737/757), Air France (Boeing 737), Air Hong Kong (Boeing 747), Air Kilroe (Jetstream 31), Air Littoral (Brasilia), Air Malta (Airbus A320, Boeing 737), Air Transat (TriStar, Boeing 757), Air UK (Fokker 100, BAe 146), Air UK Leisure (Boeing 737), Air 2000 (Boeing 757), Airtours (MD80, Boeing 757/767), Airworld (Airbus A320), American Airlines (Boeing 767, MD11), American Trans Air (Boeing 757, TriStar), Balkan (Airbus A320, Tu-154), BASE Regional Airlines (Jetstream 31), British Airways (Boeing 737/747/757/767, ATP, Fellowship), British Midland (Boeing 737), British World (BAe 146, One-Eleven), Britannia Airways (Boeing 757/767), Brymon Airways/BA (Dash Seven), Business Air (SAAB SF340), Caledonian (Boeing 757, DC-10, TriStar), Canada 3000 (Boeing 757), Canadian Airlines (Boeing 767), Cathay Pacific (Boeing 747), Centennial (MD80), Croatia Airlines (Boeing 737), CSA Czechoslovak Airlines (Boeing 737, Tu-134), Cyprus Airways (Airbus A310/320), Delta Air Lines (TriStar), EgyptAir (Airbus A320, Boeing 767), El Al (Boeing 757), Emirates (Airbus A310), Euro Direct (ATP, Jetstream 31), Excalibur Airways (Airbus A320), Finnair (MD80), Futura (Boeing 737), GB Airways (Boeing 737), Gill Air (Short SD3-30), Gulf Air (Boeing 767), Iberia (MD80), Interline (Jetstream 31), Istanbul Airlines (Boeing 737), Jersey European (Friendship, BAe 146), Lauda Air (Canadair Regional Jet), Leisure International (Boeing 767), LOT Polish Airlines (Boeing 737), LTE (Boeing 757), Lufthansa (Airbus A320, Boeing 737, Canadair Regional Jet), Maersk Air UK (One-Eleven), Manx Airlines (ATP, Jetstream 41), Monarch (Airbus A300/320, Boeing 757), Newair (Jetstream 31), Oasis (MD80), Onur Air (Airbus A320), Pakistan International (Boeing 747), Pegasus (Boeing 737), Regional Airlines (Jetstream J31), Royal Air (TriStar), Royal Air Maroc (Boeing 737), Ryanair (Boeing 737), SABENA (BAe 146, Boeing 737), SAS (DC-9, MD80), Singapore Airlines (Boeing 747), Spanair (MD80), Suckling Airways (Dornier Do228), Swissair (MD80), Tarom (Boeing 737, One-Eleven), TAT (Fellowship), TransLift (Airbus A320), Ukraine International (Boeing 737), World Airways (MD11).

Movements (1993): Total 136,400. Total passengers 12,852,000.

Runway: 06/24 (10,000ft/3,048m).

Radio frequencies: 118.625MHz (Tower), 119.4MHz (Approach), 121.7MHz (Ground).

Telephone: (0161) 489 3000

Operated by: Manchester Airport PLC

Milan (Linate)

Although associated with aviation from the early days of flying, the field now known as Linate was not developed as a civil airport until the 1930s, opening to traffic in 1936. Unlike Malpensa it was never intended for military use and, since the Italians were keen to employ seaplanes, the new site was also provided with an artificial lake. In Europe only Berlin/Tempelhof is situated nearer to a city centre than Linate, the latter being only six miles from the heart of Milan. This highly convenient position was certainly one of the main factors for the postwar decision to develop it in preference to Malpensa. After a comprehensive modernisation programme which consumed two years, a DC-6B of Lebanon International Airways had the distinction of becoming the first movement at the rejuvenated airport on 25 June 1960.

From September 1960 all European and domestic traffic was transferred from Malpensa, a move welcomed by travellers and airlines alike. Unfortunately this happy state of affairs was not to last. Traffic growth exceeded all expectations until Linate reached saturation point. Normally, further development work would have kept pace with the growing numbers, but because of the airport's prime location on the outskirts of the city the necessary land was just not available. Consequently, capacity problems now exist at the airport which will not be resolved until at least the first phase of the Malpensa modernisation scheme is ready for service in the 1990s. By 1991 a number of carriers had already transferred their operations, an example to be followed eventually by all international services, leaving Linate to handle only domestic schedules and those to the Mediterranean islands.

Location and access: Situated 6 miles (10km) south of Milan, which is linked to the airport by an SEA bus every 20min, the journey taking 20min to complete.
Alternatively, bus route 73 links Linate with Milan San Babila at regular intervals, taking

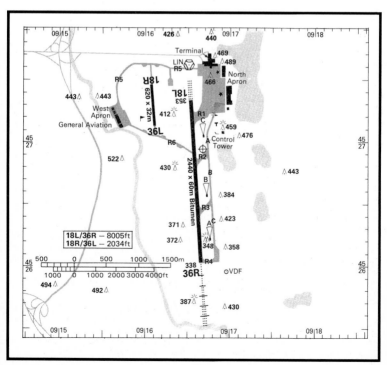

20min for the trip. Ample car parking is provided for those braving the Fiat-infested streets.

Terminal: This two-storey building contains a restaurant, buffet, bars, shops and two banks. During the course of its modernisation the whole facility was greatly enlarged.

Spectator facilities: None specifically provided, although a gallery exists in the departure area on the first floor. While there are reasonable views from here through the tinted glass of movements on the apron and elsewhere, the vantage point is of little use for photography. A more suitable location can be found around the perimeter road at a point where Runway 18L/36R is quite close.

Operators: Aer Lingus (Boeing 737), Air France (Airbus A300/320, Boeing 737, Fellowship, ATR-42), Air Littoral (Brasilia, ATR-42), Air Portugal (Airbus A310/320, Boeing 737), Air UK (Fokker 100), Alitalia (Airbus A300/321, DC-9, MD80, ATR-42), ATI (DC-9, MD80), Avianova (ATR-42), Austrian Airlines (MD80), British Airways (Boeing 737/757/767), British Airways/Maersk UK (One-Eleven), Iberia (Airbus A320, Boeing 757), Lufthansa (Airbus A320, Boeing 737, Canadair Regional Jet, Fokker 50, Dash Eight), Meridiana (MD80), Olympic Airways (Airbus A300, Boeing 737), SABENA (Boeing 737), SAS (DC-9, MD80), Swissair (Airbus A310, MD80).

Movements (1993): Total 114,157. Total passengers 9,469, 063.

Runways: 18L/36R (8,005ft/2,440m), 18R/36L (2,034ft/620m).

Radio frequencies: 118.1MHz, 119.25MHz (Tower), 132.7MHz (Approach), 126.75MHz (Departures), 121.8MHz (Ground).

Telephone: (02) 74851

Operated by: Societa Esercizi Aeroportuali (SEA)

Milan (Malpensa)

On 27 May 1907, Giovanni Caproni took to the air from a field adjacent to the sheds in which his machine, a CA-1, was built. It was not long before the small unit became the Caproni factory and the field an airstrip destined to become an international airport. A flying school was formed in 1911 which became responsible for the training of pilots taking part in the conflict between Italy and Turkey, and also in World War 1. Of those passing through the establishment during this period were the future aces Francesco Baracca and author Gabriele D'Annunzio, the latter apparently being able to continue his career as a poet while machine-gunning the Austrian trenches.

When the nation's air arm was formally created in 1923, Malpensa took a leading role by becoming the main source of trained personnel for the new force. Nevertheless, commercial flying also began at the airfield about this time, continuing until a new site was completed at Linate in 1936. During the occupation in 1943, the German army built a new runway capable of handling the increasing number of heavy transport movements required to support the ground forces. However, the creators of the strip were also responsible for its destruction at the end of April 1945, when strategically placed mines ended its short but useful life.

Soon after the war the Societa Aeroporti di Busto assumed control although it was not long before this organisation was renamed Societa Esercizi Aeroportuali (SEA), the title it retains today. Malpensa was rebuilt in 1948 to take over the role of Milan's airport, the first revenue-earning movement taking place on 21 November. For the next 12 years or so the airport coped with all the traffic, but in 1960 the completion of work at Linate brought relief. At this point most of the European and domestic flights were transferred to the new location leaving only intercontinental services at the older site.

Malpensa entered a new phase in its career in 1972 when the Italian Ministry of Transport approved a new plan to develop the airport to meet the long-term requirements towards the end of the century. Included in the project was a terminal with two satellites capable of handling 12 million passengers each year. Construction work has been carried out at a leisurely pace for completion during the 1990s, when the capacity will reach 8 million travellers. In addition, the newly built cargo facility will be capable of dealing with some 200,000 tonnes annually. In due course all international services will operate from Malpensa, the domestic traffic remaining at Linate. By 1991 a number of carriers had already transferred their operations as the first stage of the redevelopment was put into service. This included the lengthening of Runway 17R/35L.

Location and access: Situated 29 miles (46km) northwest of Milan in the Province of Varese off Autostrada A8. A regular bus links the airport with the city's central railway station, the journey time being 60min.

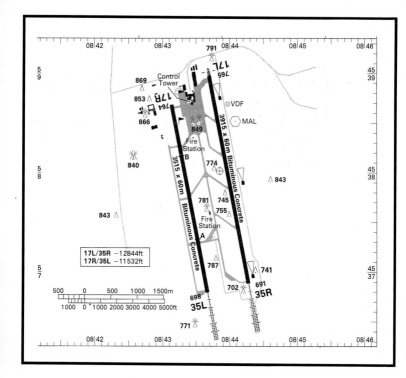

Departures are co-ordinated with incoming flights.

Terminal: Contains a restaurant, bar and shops.

Spectator facilities: The excellent first floor terrace along the front of the terminal remains in position but has been closed to the public for some years. There have been occasions when it has been reopened for short periods, but no information on the subject was forthcoming from the authority. It would therefore seem highly unlikely that a facility will be included in the plans for the new terminal whenever it is finally built. A perimeter position near to the threshold of Runway 35R provides a good vantage point for photographs, although the Italian police tend to be allergic to cameras and their owners.

Operators: Aeroflot (IL-86), Air Algerie (Boeing 737/757), Air Malta (Boeing 737), Alitalia (DC-9, MD80/11, Boeing 747), American Airlines (Boeing 767), Balkan (Airbus A320), Corse Mediterranée (ATR-42), CSA Czechoslovak Airlines (Boeing 737, ATR-72, IL-62), Delta Air Lines (Airbus A310, Boeing 767, TriStar), EgyptAir (Airbus A320), Finnair (DC-9, MD80), Japan Airlines (Boeing 747), KLM (Airbus A310, Boeing 737, Fokker 100), LOT Polish Airlines (Boeing 737), Malev (Boeing 737), Meridiana (DC-9, MD80), Middle East Airlines (Airbus A310, Boeing 707), Olympic Airways (Boeing 737), Regional Airlines (SAAB SF340), South African Airways (Boeing 747), Trans World (Boeing 747/767), Tunis Air (Airbus A320, Boeing 727), Turkish Airlines (Boeing 737), United Airlines (Boeing 747/767), Varig (Boeing 747/767).

Movements (1993): Total 37,645. Total passengers 4,940, 119.

Runways: 17L/35R (12,844ft/3,915m), 17R/35L (11,532ft/3,515m).

Radio frequencies: 119.0MHz, 128.35MHz (Tower), 132.7MHz (Approach), 126.75MHz (Departures), 121.9MHz (Ground).

Telephone: (02) 74851

Operated by: Societa Esercizi Aeroportuali

Munich

When Riem became operational as Munich's airport in 1939, it was considered to be one of the most up-to-date in the world. It quickly became used as a hub for flights to south and southeast Germany, an activity which continued throughout the war. After remaining relatively undamaged during this period, on 9 April 1945 it was almost completely destroyed by air raids. A month or so later, America became the occupying power in the area, whereupon units of the USAF were stationed at Riem. Control of the partially restored airport was handed back to the Germans in 1948, with the City of Munich and the State of Bavaria each taking a 50% share. In the following year a concrete runway was laid, but as traffic and the size of the airliners steadily grew in the 1950s it became necessary to extend the 6,233ft (1,900m) strip to 8,530ft (2,600m) before the end of the decade.

By the 1960s it was apparent that the limitation of Riem's capacity was becoming a serious problem, but expansion was not possible due to the existence of urban areas on three sides of the airport. Safety was also a major consideration because the flight paths passed over these densely populated residential areas, which were therefore subjected to unacceptable noise levels. A search for a new site began, a lengthy process which attracted 26,332 objections from private individuals and 180 requests from various authorities. Eventually, approval was received in July 1979, but almost immediately building work was suspended to deal with legal actions arising from another 5,724 objections. Four years then passed before the project could really get under way in 1986, with the completion planned for 1992.

From the very beginning of the scheme, it was proposed that a system of parallel runways would be featured in the design. This ensured that Munich 2 would have adequate capacity in the long term with very good operational conditions. Noise levels are reduced by keeping the runways a

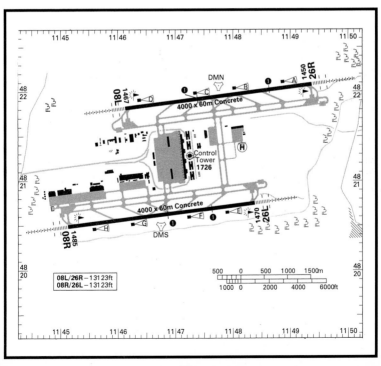

08L/26R – 13123ft
08R/26L – 13123ft

considerable distance apart, while the length largely eliminates the use of reverse thrust. This layout allowed the airport complex to be located in the centre with surface access by rail and road from the west. Fast turn-offs from both runways lead to a series of taxiways linked to an extensive apron area capable of accommodating 48 parked aircraft, 20 of them on airbridges. Most of the remainder park at boarding stations, a unique system devised for the remote stands. Buses are used to carry passengers to the aircraft, but boarding is completed under cover, a useful feature which protects travellers from the weather during the often protracted process. The terminal consists of four linked modules, each operating as an independent unit with all the facilities needed. Altogether, the quartet was designed to handle up to 12 million passengers annually, a figure already reached in its short career after the formal opening on 17 May 1992.

Lufthansa has established its second major maintenance base in Germany by constructing a hangar at Munich which is the largest in Europe. Elsewhere on the airport, a cargo centre has been built with a start-up annual capacity of 270,000 tonnes. With a catchment area stretching into Italy, Austria, Slovakia and the German states, Munich is set to become one of the most important facilities for such business.

Location and access: Situated 17 miles (28.5km) northeast of the centre of Munich in the Erdinger Moos. Links are made with the Munich-Deggendorf autobahn, while the western approach connects with the district FS44 road. To the east, the airport's ring road joins autobahn A92, a network due to be extended to the A94 in 1995. A new rapid transit line (S8) connects with the Munich integrated transport system and the German Federal Railways, taking about 38min from the airport station to Munich Hof. Trains run every 20min for most of the 24hrs. Bus 635 runs from the terminal to Freising station for connections with trains to Regensburg, Passau and Dresden.
Spectator facilities: A viewing area complete with mound has been provided which gives good views over the aprons, while organised tours of the airport depart from the spectators' area several times on Saturdays and Sundays at a cost of DM10.
Operators: Aeroflot (Tu-154), Aero Lloyd (MD80), African Safaris (DC-8/10), Air Belgium (Boeing 737), Air Berlin (Boeing 737), Air Charter (Airbus A300/320), Air Dolomiti (ATR-42, Dash Eight), Air Engiadina (Dornier Do228/328), Air Europa (Boeing 737), Air France (Airbus A320, Boeing 737), Air Holland (Boeing 757), Air Lanka (TriStar), Air Malta (Boeing 737, Airbus A320), Air Mauritius (Boeing 767), Air Portugal (Boeing 737, Airbus A320), Air UK (BAe 146, Fokker 100), Air 2000 (Boeing 757), Alitalia (DC-9, MD80), American Airlines (Boeing 767), Austrian Airlines (MD80), Avianova (ATR-42), Balair CTA (MD80, Airbus A310), Balkan (Tu-154), British Airways (Boeing 737/757), British Midland (Boeing 737), Britannia Airways (Boeing 757), BWIA International (TriStar), Canadian Airlines (Boeing 767, DC-10), Condor (Boeing 737/757/767), Croatia Airlines (Boeing 737), Crossair (SAAB SF340/2000, Fokker 50), Cyprus Airways (Airbus A320), Delta Air Lines (Boeing 767, TriStar), Deutsche BA (Fokker 100, SAAB SF340/2000, Boeing 737), EgyptAir (Boeing 767), Eurowings (ATR-42/72), Finnair (DC-9, MD80), Garuda (Boeing 747), Germania (Boeing 737), GB Airways (Boeing 737), Hapag-Lloyd (Boeing 737, Airbus A310), Iberia (Airbus A320, DC-9, MD80, Boeing 757), Icelandair (Boeing 757), Interot (Dash Eight), Istanbul Airlines (Boeing 727/737), Japan Airlines (Boeing 747), KLM (Boeing 737), Lauda Air (Boeing 737/767, Canadair Regional Jet), Lufthansa (Boeing 737/747, Airbus A300/310/320/321/340), Fokker 50, Canadair Regional Jet), LTU (TriStar, Boeing 757/767, MD11), Luxair (Fokker 50), Malaysian Airlines (Boeing 747), Martinair (Boeing 767), Malev (Boeing 737), Meridiana (DC-9), Monarch (Airbus A320, Boeing 757), Nordic East (DC-9), Olympic Airways (Airbus A300, Boeing 737), Palair Macedonia (Fokker 100), Royal Air Maroc (Boeing 727/737), SABENA (Boeing 737), SAS (DC-9, MD80), Sobelair (Boeing 737), Sterling European (Boeing 727), Swissair (MD80, Fokker 100), Tarom (One-Eleven, Tu-154), TAT (Fokker 100), TUR European (Boeing 727), Transavia (Boeing 737), Turkish Airlines (Boeing 737, Airbus A310), Tyrolean (Dash Eight), ZAS Airline of Egypt (MD80).
Movements (1993): Total 181,000. Total passengers 12,732,000.
Runways: 08L/26R (13,123ft/4,000m), 08R/26L (13,123ft/4,000m).
Radio frequencies: 118.7MHz, 120.2MHz (Tower), 128.025MHz, 120.775MHz (Approach).
Telephone: (089) 975 00
Operated by: Munich Airport Authority

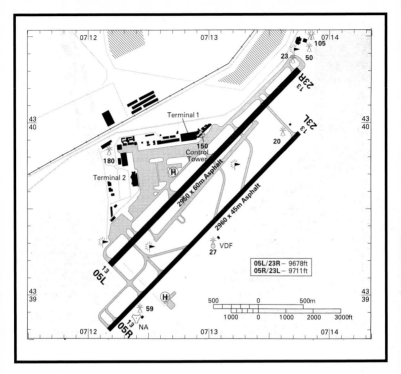

Map labels: 07|12, 07|13, 07|14, 105, 23, 50, 23R, 13, Terminal 1, 43/40, 23L, 13, 150, Control Tower, 20, 180, H, Terminal 2, 2950 x 60m Asphalt, 2960 x 45m Asphalt, VDF, 27, 13, 05L, 05L/23R – 9678ft, 05R/23L – 9711ft, 43/39, H, 59, 13, 05R, NA, 500, 0, 500m, 1000, 0, 1000, 2000, 3000ft, 07|12, 07|13, 07|14

Nice (Riviera)

Generally thought of as a holiday centre, Nice became the scene of some of the earliest flying to take place in Europe. As early as 1901 the French pioneer Capitaine Louis Ferber carried out the first tests with his machine, which was suspended from the arm of a structure resembling a tower crane. The tethered creation was then able to propel itself in a circular movement in a similar manner to a roundabout at a fairground. Nine years later the town organised a series of large aviation meetings for European aviators, offering attractive prizes for outstanding successes. At these both speed and altitude records were established with machines such as the Antoinette.

By the early 1920s a site was earmarked for use as an aerodrome and a 700m grass runway was laid with its western end near to Nice racecourse. Most of the aerodrome's activity was devoted to sport flying between its opening and the early 1930s, but by

1936 the French carrier Potez Aéro-Service had introduced scheduled services between Nice, Toulouse, Bordeaux and Corsica using Potez 56 airliners. Noting the success of this enterprise, plans were drawn up for the development of the airport but, before any action could be taken on the proposals, World War 2 tended to move it down the scale of priorities.

For much of the war there was no change at the site, but in 1944 the Allies invaded southern France. This led to the construction of a hard runway over 4,000ft (1,219m) in length principally for the use of the logistics base which had been set up in support of the Italian campaign. After the war the strip proved a useful asset, encouraging Air France to start scheduled services. Development was considered to be in the public interest so work started on strengthening the runway, which at the same time was also extended to 5,577ft (1,700m). By the end of the first year the airport was able to report that 34,267 passengers had used the facilities and that

Above: KLM and SABENA 737s share the apron in front of Nice's Terminal 1 International.
N.Huffschmitt/Nice-Riviera Airport

there had been 5,091 aircraft movements.

By 1949 not only was the French flag carrier operating from Nice, but both BEA and Swissair were in evidence. Routes to London and Geneva therefore resulted, while long-haul sectors were introduced to such unlikely places as Tehran, Brazzaville and Saigon. From 1946 the airport had taken the name of Nice-le-Var, but in 1955 the present identity of Côte d'Azur was adopted. Now officially recognised as a regional centre, at the end of the next year over 500,000 passengers were recorded for the first time. Fortunately this growth had been anticipated several years earlier when work had begun on the development of a complex for the French Riviera capable of meeting the demands of the expanding holiday industry. On 2 December 1957 the new Nice airport was opened.

Although utilising the same site, the existing buildings had been replaced by a smart new terminal and freight centre. Despite being adequate for the period, as the larger airliners began to appear so expansion became necessary once again, until by 1969 the terminal had been enlarged twice to enable it to cope with an annual capacity of 2.5 million. Naturally the runway also needed some more stretching if it was to handle the new types of aircraft, so by 1973 it had grown to 9,840ft (3,000m). Unfortunately the limits for any further increase in size had almost been reached due to the compactness of the area, bordered by the sea to the south, the city of Nice to the north and east plus the Var river in the west.

Studies were begun to find a solution to this difficult problem which culminated in the decision to build a second runway on land reclaimed from the sea. It was a bold step and one which took some governmental thought, but on 24 December 1974 approval was given for the scheme. For several years a constant stream of lorries shuttled between nearby Le Collet de Cremat quarry and the airport laden with the material needed for the infill until finally the enormous task was completed with the opening of the new south runway on 23 October 1983. The year also saw 4 million passengers for the first time which helped to provide the incentive to start the first stages of Terminal 2 in April 1985. Built to a modern design, when opened two years or so later it took over the handling of the domestic traffic, which alone generated an annual total of well over 2 million passengers.

To the south of the site, a stretch of land between the runways and the sea may also be developed. A geological survey has been carried out to determine the feasibilty of the scheme. The reclaimed land would be used for facilities such as fuel storage tanks and other amenities.

Once the new accommodation was on line, thoughts turned towards the next project which was duly begun in May 1990. This time it was the turn of the much-modified original building now known as Terminal 1. One of the first steps taken was to construct a new roof over the entire complex thereby allowing the dismantling of the previous cover and a start to be made on the revised interior layout. To facilitate this activity and to allow the smooth running of the airport to continue, a temporary building was erected alongside the south side of Terminal 2. Known as Zone 3, the structure was built to the same standards as its permanent neighbours, but by using new techniques was ready for service in five months. It then took over most of the check-in activities, enabling work to proceed apace on the virtually new international Terminal 1 which was designed to have an annual capacity of 5 million passengers when operational in 1994.

At this point the workforce did not become unemployed because it was then intended to proceed with a second module for Terminal 2. In the meantime a new freight complex was created on the west side of the site. When opened in 1991, its capacity of 50,000 tonnes more than doubled the previous handling capacity of the airport.

Nice is now France's second airport and is preparing to cope with 10 million passengers by the turn of the century. This target is by no means impossible in view of the campaign already under way to promote the area as the southern European gateway. Intensive efforts are being made to attract North American and Asian carriers to the Côte d'Azur which are already proving successful.

The new Mercantour Tunnel will result in a one-and-a-half-hour drive between Nice and Turin by the year 2000. Once this access is available, the airport will no longer exclusively serve the Riviera region, but also northern Italy. By the year 2010 this will produce a catchment area of some 10 million potential passengers, so a start has already been made on the necessary expansion plans. There will be a need for the airport to act as a hub for long-haul services with European connections readily available. Likewise, the terminals will no longer be allocated on a geographical basis, but by individual airlines instead. They will also handle both international and domestic traffic, while a gallery is to be built between the buildings for easier transfers. Ultimately,

therefore, there will in effect be one only terminal, although detailed design work has yet to be finalised. Upon completion of the first phase of the expansion, the airport's capacity will rise by some 4 million passengers annually.

Location and access: Situated 4 miles (7km) southwest of Nice alongside the main coast road and adjacent to RN7. There is a bus service from Nice (Avenue Felix Faure) with a journey time of 20min to Terminal 1 and 23min to Terminal 2. Car parks are available, but invariably busy. A free shuttle bus links the terminals at a frequency depending on demand.

Terminals: Terminal 1 is located on the northern side of the apron and will handle international movements when fully operational at the end of 1994. On the western edge of the site, Terminal 2 has two levels, with most of the services located on the upper departure floor. There are three fixed airbridges connecting the building with the aircraft.

Spectator facilities: A useful open-air terrace along the front of Terminal 1 is open between 10.00hrs and 18.00hrs. This gives good views of the apron's contents, but its south-facing aspect produces problems for photographers, although it does not make photography impossible. The access roads to Terminal 2 also offer possibilities for shots of aircraft on the near taxiways, with afternoons producing the best results bearing in mind the position of the sun. There are alternatives to the east of the airport, where the taxiway passes very close to the Promenade des Anglais, but once again the sun is not co-operative. A more useful spot is located at the mouth of the River Var. It is actually a part of the large CAP3000 shopping complex, so there is adequate parking and refreshments are on hand when required. From this comfortable vantage point all movements can be seen and photography is well within the scope of a 200mm lens. Conducted tours of the airport and a retired Caravelle are organised upon requests made at least one week in advance. Normally parties total between 15 and 50 people. Information can be obtained by telephoning 93 21 30 09 Monday to Friday.

Operators: Air Afrique (Airbus A310), Air Algerie (Boeing 737), Air Canada (Boeing 767), Air Club International (Boeing 767), Air France (Airbus A300/310/320, Boeing 737, Fellowship, Air Gabon (Boeing 747), Air Inter (Airbus A300/320/330), Air Liberte (Airbus

A300), Air Littoral (Brasilia, ATR-42), Air Portugal (Airbus A320, Boeing 737), Air Toulouse (Caravelle), Air UK (BAe 146, Fokker 100), Alitalia (MD80), AOM French Airlines (MD80), Austrian Airlines (MD80), Brit Air (ATR-42, SAAB SF340), British Airways (Fellowship, Boeing 737/757), British Midland (DC-9, Fokker 70), Corse Mediterranée (ATR-72, Fokker 100), Crossair (SAAB SF340/2000), Delta Air Lines (Boeing 767, TriStar), Deutsche BA (Fokker 100), El Al (Boeing 757), Emirates (Airbus S300/310), Eurowings (ATR-42/72), Finnair (DC-9), Heli Air Monaco (Ecureuil), Heli Inter Riviera (Ecureuil, Dauphin, JetRanger), Iberia (MD80), KLM (Fokker 100, Boeing 737), Kuwait Airways (Airbus A310), LOT Polish Airlines (Boeing 737), Lufthansa (Airbus A320, Boeing 737), Luxair (Boeing 737, Fokker 50), Meridiana (ATR-42), Middle East Airlines (Airbus A310), Proteus (Beech 1900), Regional Airlines (SAAB SF340), Royal Air Maroc (Boeing 727/737), SABENA (Boeing 737), SAS (DC-9, MD80), Sunline (Gulfstream 1), Swissair (MD80, Fokker 100), TAT European (Brasilia, Beech 1900, ATR-42/72), Tower Air (Boeing 747), Tunis Air (Airbus A300/320, Boeing 727/737), Turkish Airlines (Boeing 737).

Movements (1993): Total 126,283 (commercial 74,114, private 15,567, helicopters 36,602). Total passengers 5,940,220.

Runways: 05L/23R (9,678ft/2,950m), 05R/23L (9,711ft/2,960m).

Radio frequencies: 118.7MHz, 121.275MHz (Tower), 120.25MHz, 120.85MHz, 124.175MHz (Approach), 123.15MHz (Ground).

Telephone: Nice 93 21 30 30

Operated by: Riviera Airports

Oslo (Fornebu)

Although chosen as the site for a future airport in September 1934, it was June 1939 before Fornebu was opened. During that first summer KLM, ABA and Lufthansa all started scheduled services, although the national carrier, DNL, continued to operate from the neighbouring seaplane base at Gressholmen. This situation was not to last. Only a very brief civilian life was enjoyed before the German forces arrived in the spring of the following year. Thereafter the facilities were used by the invaders for military purposes until the end of the war in 1945.

After a period of renovation, the airport resumed its civilian status in February 1946. Expansion was necessary through the ensuing years, culminating in the opening of a new passenger terminal in 1964. This proved adequate for the next decade or so, but by the early 1980s plans were being prepared to bring Fornebu up to modern standards. A new international building was subsequently constructed on the north side of the main complex for the use of departing international passengers, the latest addition (Pier C) being opened in May 1988. Two satellites (A and B) are connected to the main building by covered walkways, while another was added to the west end of Pier C.

In the meantime the original terminal has also been extensively modernised to give much more space in the waiting area, together with a large shopping centre plus improved catering and bar facilities. In late 1991 the two resident handling agents, SAS and Braathens, were allocated their own domestic arrival/departure halls. At the same time, arriving international passengers began to use a new facility, a development that was designed to ease the traffic flow through the airport still further.

Built on land bordered by the sea on three sides, Fornebu still has the useful ability to handle seaplane traffic in addition to that more usually found at airports. This geographical feature on the other hand has restricted the runway lengths, so all transatlantic movements are handled at Gardemoen, some 32 miles (51km) from the city. With the completion of the latest modernisation and expansion programme at Fornebu, there seemed little likelihood of a new site taking over as Norway's major international gateway in the foreseeable future. However, since the 1960s there have been plans to construct a brand-new airport, but it was not until 1988 that the government actually decided where it would be located, assuming it ever materialised. There seemed little urgency and in any case, no action could be taken until the necessary funds were forthcoming, a fact guaranteed to encourage more prolonged debate. Opponents of the scheme were given fresh hope during 1989 when the traffic volume at Fornebu dropped, but this was shortlived due to the trend reversing in the following year. It has now been decided to go-ahead with the construction plans at the new location which should be operational in 1998. In the meantime the Norwegian Government is considering the instigation of

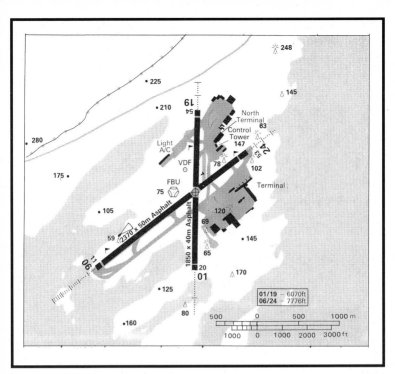

01/19 — 6070ft
06/24 — 7776ft

a ban between 18.00 and 06.00 on aircraft not complying with the Stage Three noise conditions. This plan was announced during 1994 to take effect in the following year, but after representations the introduction was deferred pending further talks.

Location and access: Situated 5 miles (8km) southwest of Oslo via E18 (Drammen) road. A bus runs every 10min between the Central railway station and the airport with a journey time of 25min.

Terminal: A four-storey building, the ground and first floors are devoted to arrivals and departures respectively, with the second containing refreshment facilities and administration, the latter also taking the entire top floor.

Spectator facilities: None are provided, although from the second floor buffet area a limited view is possible. On the other hand, the car park offers excellent opportunities for photography of both arriving and departing aircraft, while the presence of float planes on the adjacent lake is an added attraction. Within easy walking

distance is the general aviation area and the hangars used by Braathens and Fred Olsen. Fornebu is worth visiting if in the area, but the likely rewards do not really justify a special sortie.

Operators: Aeroflot (Tu-154), Air France (Boeing 737), Air Malta (Boeing 737), Air Portugal (Boeing 737), Air Stord (Super King Air), Alitalia (DC-9, MD80), Braathens (Boeing 737), British Airways (Boeing 737/757), Coast Air (Twin Otter), Delta Air Lines (Airbus A310, Boeing 767, TriStar), Deutsche BA (Fokker 100), Finnair (DC-9, MD80), Fred Olsen (Electra), Icelandair (Boeing 737/757), KLM (Boeing 737), LOT Polish Airlines (Boeing 737), Lufthansa (Boeing 737, Fokker 50, Canadair Regional Jet), Maersk Air (Boeing 737), Muk Air (Short SD3-30), Premiair (Airbus A320, DC-10), SABENA (Boeing 737), SAS (DC-9, MD80, Boeing 767, Fokker 50), Sterling European (Boeing 727), Sun-Air (Jetstream 31), Talair (SAAB SF340), Wideroe (Dash Seven/Eight, Twin Otter).

Movements (1993): Total 138,630 (scheduled 111,181/charter 1,353). Total

passengers 7,617,000.
Runways: 06/24 (7,776ft/2,370m), 01/19 (6,070ft/1,850m).
Radio frequencies: 118.1MHz (Tower), 120.45MHz (Approach), 119.65MHz (Departure), 121.7MHz (Ground).
Telephone: (67) 59 33 40
Operated by: Civil Aviation Administration

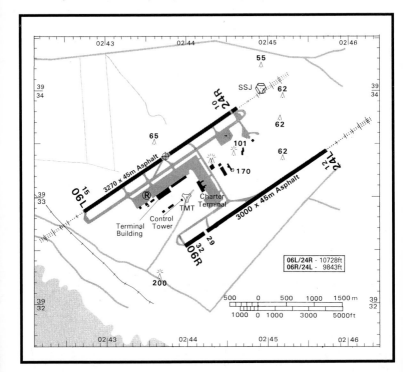

Palma

Before tourists descended upon the island of Mallorca in their millions, the airfield at Son Bonet was quite capable of handling the modest flow of traffic, despite possessing only two grass runways offering a maximum length of 4,900ft/1,493m. As tour operators began to sell ITs in ever-increasing numbers, so the Spanish authorities recognised the need for some development. With little scope for any major changes at the existing site, it was decided to utilise the military base to the east of Palma, which had the benefit of being near to the coast with no obstructions to the south. In 1966 a scheduled service terminal was duly opened at Son San Juan to be followed in 1972 by another for the use of the charter flights. Subsequently the

airport's apron areas have been greatly extended to accommodate the ever-growing number of airliners, most of which have to park on stands away from the buildings. Usually one terminal is sufficient for the winter season, when movements drop away dramatically. Despite the encouraging sounds made by the travel industry, Mallorca is not a haven for sun-seekers at that time of year, although it does enjoy higher temperatures than northern Europe.

For many years Palma has managed with just one 10,500ft/3,200m runway, although in the 1970s a second was laid but never used. Instead it became a parking spot for the withdrawn airliners such as the Coronados of Spantax and DC-8s of the defunct TAE. However, in the early 1980s another attempt began to extend the airport, the result being that a brand-new runway

Above: Icelandair operates a scheduled service to Palma using its 737-400s, one of which is TF-FID. *AJW*

was ready for service by the end of 1987. Strangely enough, during the period of construction little thought seems to have been given to the existence of the hotels and houses on the nearby coastal strip, many of which are directly under the flight path. Any objections went unheard until the new creation was ready for service, whereupon pressure was brought to bear to restrict the runway's use to off-peak periods. This of course defeated the whole object of the exercise, although it had already been accepted that it would be used only for northerly take-offs or southerly landings to reduce the noise nuisance. As a result there was little relief for the chronic congestion suffered by the airport during the summer peaks.

In anticipation of the opening of the new runway, plans had also been made for the erection of a more suitable control tower. Several years passed as the work proceeded at a leisurely pace, but when eventually completed in 1987 it gave the controllers a much improved view from their elevated position. This was long overdue because throughout the growth of the civilian facilities, the military presence has remained at the northern end of the runway. Spanish Air Force aircraft are therefore quite common, ranging from fighters to search and rescue types, so the mix has to be carefully monitored.

Location and access: Situated 4.5 miles (7km) east of Palma, to which it is linked by motorway. Bus route 17 links the city centre (Plaza Espania) with the airport every 30min. Otherwise the easiest method is by taxi or hire car.

Terminals: The two buildings are similar in layout and have the usual buffet facilities. These are generally inadequate to cope with the crowds of passengers waiting for their flights. Refreshments are also expensive. The charter terminal in particular can become very hot and crowded, although there is a small external section to the buffet if there is a desire to seek fresher air.

Spectator facilities: Palma once had a terrace on the first floor which overlooked the apron used by the scheduled flights. This is no more, of course, and neither is anything provided in the charter building, although its large glass panels do give departing passengers a limited view across the apron. Since a collection of international finger marks decorates these panes, the chances of a reasonable photograph are poor. A narrow field of vision is just possible from the outdoor buffet area, but is hardly worth the effort. Better vantage points both for viewing and photography are to be found around the boundaries. When runway 06L is in use, good landing shots can be obtained from the shore to the west of C'an Pastilla. This town also has several hotels, such as the Luz, which are in a convenient position for viewing all movements on 06L/24R from the comfort of the balcony. A room with a westerly aspect is necessary. Elsewhere, a track parallel with the northwest side of this runway offers excellent opportunities for take-off shots in the afternoons. This spot can be reached by hired cycle via Manacor after about 20min of leisurely pedalling. Several years ago, care was necessary to avoid the unwanted attentions of those keen on collecting valuables from tourists. This situation has now improved, but it is still wise to carry cameras and the like in plastic carrier bags rather than in more readily identifiable containers. In the mornings a trip to the side of 06R/24L is worth the exercise, again with the prospect of some excellent landing or take-off shots, depending on the wind direction.

Operators: Scheduled services by Air Algerie (Friendship, Boeing 727), Air Belgium (Boeing 737/757), Air Europa (Boeing 737/757), Air Inter (Airbus A300/320), Aviaco (DC9, MD80), British Midland (DC-9, Fokker 70, Boeing 737), Centennial (MD80), Condor (Boeing 737/757, DC-10), CSA Czechoslovak Airlines (Tu-154), Iberia (Airbus A320, Boeing 727/757, MD80), Icelandair (Boeing 737), LTU (Boeing 757/767, TriStar, MD11), Lufthansa (Airbus A300/310/320, Boeing

737), Luxair (Boeing 737), Monarch Airlines (Airbus A300/320), Spanair (MD80), Swissair (MD80), Transavia (Boeing 737), Viva Air (Boeing 737). **Charter and IT operators** include Aer Lingus (Boeing 737), Aero Lloyd (DC-9, MD80), Air Berlin (Boeing 737), Air Charter International (Boeing 727/737), Air Holland (Boeing 757), Air Liberte (MD80), Air Provence (Gulfstream 1), Air Toulouse (Caravelle, Boeing 737), Airtours (MD80, Airbus A320, Boeing 757), Airworld (Airbus A320), Air UK Leisure (Boeing 737), Air 2000 (Airbus A320, Boeing 757), Austrian Airlines (MD80), Balair CTA (MD80, DC-10, Airbus A310), Britannia Airways (Boeing 757/767), British Airways (Boeing 737), British World (One-Eleven, BAe 146), Caledonian Airways (Airbus A320, Boeing 757, TriStar), Condor (Boeing 737/757/767, DC-10), EuroBelgian Airlines (Boeing 737), European Airlines (Airbus A300), Excalibur Airways (Airbus A320), Futura (Boeing 737), Germania (Boeing 737), Hapag-Lloyd (Boeing 737, Airbus A310), LTE (Boeing 757), Maersk Air (Boeing 737), Martinair (Boeing 767), Oasis (MD80), Palmair Flightline (BAe 146), Premiair (Airbus A320, DC-10), Sabre Airways (Boeing 737), Skyjet (DC-10), Sobelair (Boeing 737), Transavia (Boeing 737/757), TransLift (Airbus A320), Transwede (MD80).

Movements (1993): Total 105,500. Total passengers 12,429,000.

Runways: 06L/24R (10,728ft/3,270m), 06R/24L (9,843ft/3,000m).

Radio frequencies: 118.3MHz (Tower), 118.95MHz, 119.15MHz (Approach), 121.7MHz (Ground).

Telephone: Palma 26 46 28

Operated by: Spanish National Airports

Paris
(Charles de Gaulle)

Research into a suitable spot for another Paris airport began in 1957 with the knowledge that Le Bourget could not be extended any further and its capacity was only 3 million passengers. Already Orly was being developed, but even there expansion possibilities were not unlimited. Once again the planners were very fortunate in finding a large area of land in a region known as the Plain of Old France, situated only 20km from the city. Just how sparsely populated the site was before construction work started in 1966 was confirmed when only one farm had to be demolished in the interests of progress. During the new airport's early days it took the local name of Roissy, but this was dropped at the time of the opening in favour of Charles de Gaulle (CDG).

At the first stage in its development the new complex was centred around the terminal and its seven outlying satellite buildings, a cargo facility and maintenance areas belonging to UTA and Air France. When designing the passenger accommodation, three particular requirements were borne in mind by the planners. Walking distance between car or coach and the aircraft should be as short as possible; loading, unloading and servicing must be both simple and speedy; and, finally, the building had to be able to handle multiples of wide-bodied aircraft without congestion. A circular configuration was chosen to meet these demands while the

satellites were wedge-shaped and capable of each dealing with four aircraft at one time. Passengers reach the gates via underground walkways equipped with travelators, a mode of transport used extensively within the main building, where escalators also proliferate.

All this resulted in an impressively futuristic layout, but in the light of experience one not particularly beneficial for the operators. Originally it was planned that five of these conglomerations would be built as growth dictated, but as the airport capacity began to reach saturation point in the late 1970s, construction was started on the second unit, located in the southeast section of the site. When completed it was intended for the use of Air France, so the carrier collaborated with the design at an early stage. Learning from experience, this time the configuration was more conventional, comprising a pair of elliptical units interconnected by a service road. Opened on 28 March 1982, the newcomer was considered an improvement on its predecessor, which offered no opportunities for expansion. For several years Terminals 2A and 2B were adequate, but in 1987 work began on the second pair in the series of identical buildings to be provided as traffic demands. When completed in 1990, the first became 2D and was allocated for the use of the growing number of commuter aircraft feeding the airport. Previously these were forced to park on a distant apron from which buses took the passengers to the terminal. Generally this was no longer the case because stands were available adjacent to the building. Meanwhile, work

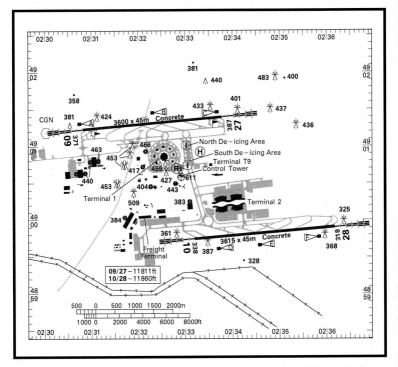

```
09/27 – 11811ft
10/28 – 11860ft
```

continued on unit 2C to meet the planned service date in 1993. Unlike its three companions it has departures and arrivals on different levels, allowing better security control.

Design and initial earth-moving work for the future CDG-3 complex was already under way in 1990. It marks a new phase in the architectural development of air terminals, yet retains the principle of the speedy throughput of passengers, while at the same time directly serving a larger number of apron stands. Each of the individual units will be considerably larger than those at CDG-2, being about 1,300ft (400m) long compared with 800ft (250m). There will also be a pier extending from each end allowing almost twice as many airbridges to be installed. The overall result will be a 25% increase in capacity, but for a similar amount of traffic, the new terminals will give a third more space for passengers. In addition, work has started on the future F unit of Terminal 2 which is due to open to the public in 1997. Arrangements have been made for the application of the EU's open

borders agreement in all the terminals as soon as it comes into force.

Back in the 1960s it was anticipated that CDG would have a comprehensive system of runways, but it was some years before the single strip was supplemented by a second, constructed to become operational in 1982. An intricate network of taxiways exists, however, which, together with the fast turn-off points, is of considerable help in keeping the traffic moving smoothly. Nevertheless, the preliminary excavations for a third runway were progressing in 1994. It is to be located in the southern part of the site parallel to the existing pair. If CDG is to maintain its present growth rate, this major project is considered essential.

Location and access: Situated 14.5 miles (23km) northeast of Paris with access from the A1 motorway (toll-free from the city). A major new highway is due to link CDG with the EuroDisney theme park, plus a four-lane road to the twin towns of Cergy-Pontoise by 1995. A rail service connects the airport with the centre of Paris at Gare du Nord, taking about 30min for the trip. A new interchange station was due to open in November 1994, giving passengers easy access to the TGV high-speed train continental network, plus suburban and road services all in the same place. It is estimated that with around 40 trains running every day through the station by the year 2000, some 2 million travellers a year will be using the interchange to switch between different modes of transport. Using the RATP bus route 350 the journey to the airport takes 40min from either Gare du Nord, Gare de l'Est or Nation. In addition, Air France coaches travel between the city (Maillot) and CDG but are more expensive than the normal services. The airline's coaches also provide the facility for travel between Orly and CDG, a journey which takes 50min.

Terminals: Five floors of Terminal 1 are used by the public, with one allocated to various amenities such as shops and buffets. Terminals 2A, 2B and 2D on the other hand are on one level which corresponds approximately to the height of an aircraft's cabin. Terminal 2C has reverted to the system for segregating arrivals and departures. The two complexes are about one mile apart but a frequent free shuttle bus links them.

Spectator facilities: In its early career Terminal 1 was blessed with a terrace, but, like many others, this has been closed. From the road around the building somewhat restricted views can be obtained and even an occasional photograph, but attempting the latter usually arouses the interest of the prowling gendarmerie. This will quickly be confirmed by the piercing sound of a whistle. Around the Terminal 2 complex, the service road also provides the basis for some shots, providing discretion is used. As an alternative, the car park at the Zone Technique has been employed successfully for some years and from this vantage point some good shots can be obtained of aircraft using Terminal 1. Probably because of the airport's growing popularity with visitors, the local law has taken a less tolerant attitude in recent times. Nevertheless, despite all the problems, it is still possible to photograph some interesting subjects at Charles de Gaulle.

Operators: Aer Lingus (Boeing 737, Fokker 50), Aeroflot (Airbus A310, IL-86, Tu-134/154), Aerolineas Argentinas (Boeing 747), Air Afrique (Airbus A310, DC-10), Air Canada (Boeing 747/767), Air China (Boeing 747), Air France (Airbus A300/310/320 /321/340, Boeing 737/747/767, ATR-42, Concorde), Air Gabon (Boeing 747), Air India (Boeing 747), Air Inter (ATR-42), Air Lanka (TriStar), Air Madagascar (Boeing 747), Air Mauritius (Airbus A340, Boeing 747), Air Teranga (DC-10), Air UK (BAe 146, Fokker 50/100), Alitalia (DC-9, MD80), All Nippon (Boeing 747), Alyemda (Airbus A310), ATI (MD80), Avianca (Boeing 767), British Airways (Boeing 737/767, Dash Seven/Eight, Fokker 100, ATR-42), British Midland (DC-9, Boeing 737, Fokker 100), Cameroon Airlines (Boeing 747), Canadian Airlines (Boeing

Above :
Cubana's aircraft are seen at only a few European airports, Paris/Orly being one of the gateways. The schedules are maintained by IL-62s such as CU-T1215. *AJW*

767), Cathay Pacific (Boeing 747), Compagnie Aéronautique Européenne (Metro), Crossair (Avro RJ85, SAAB SF340/2000), CSA Czechoslovak Airlines (Boeing 737, IL-62), Cyprus Airways (Airbus A310/320), Deutsche BA (SAAB SF340), El Al (Boeing 747/757), Emirates (Airbus A310), EVA Air (Boeing 747), Eurowings (ATR-42), Finnair (DC-9, MD80), Garuda (Boeing 747, MD11), Gulf Air (Boeing 767), Japan Airlines (Boeing 747), Kenya Airways (Airbus A310), KLM (Airbus A310, Boeing 737, Fokker 50), Korean Air (Boeing 747), Kuwait Airways (Airbus A300/310), LAM Linhas Aereas de Moçambique (Boeing 767), Lithuanian Airlines (Yak-42), LOT Polish Airlines (Boeing 737, Tu-154), Lufthansa (Airbus A320, Boeing 737, Fokker 50, Dash Eight, Canadair Regional Jet), Luxair (Fokker 50), Malaysian Airlines (Boeing 747), Malev (Boeing 737, Tu-154), Manx Airlines (Jetstream 41), Meridiana (DC-9, BAe 146), Northwest Airlines (Boeing

747), Philippine Airlines (Boeing 747), Qantas (Boeing 747), SABENA (Boeing 737), SAS (DC-9, MD80), Saudia (TriStar), Singapore Airlines (Boeing 747), Sudan Airways (Airbus A310), Swissair (MD80, Fokker 100), Syrian Arab (Boeing 727/747), Thai Airways International (Boeing 747), Trans World (Boeing 747/767), Tyrolean Airways (Dash Eight), Ukraine International (Boeing 737), United Airlines (Boeing 727/747/767), Varig (Boeing 747, MD11).

Movements (1993): Total 303,710. Total passengers 26,115,800.

Runways: 09/27 (11,811ft/3,600m), 10/28 (11,860ft/3,615m).

Radio frequencies: 119.25MHz, 120.65MHz, 125.325MHz (Tower), 121.15MHz, 119.85MHz (Approach), 124.35MHz, 133.375MHz (Departure), 121.6MHz (Ground).

Telephone: (1) 48 62 12 12

Operated by: Aéroports de Paris

Paris (Orly)

Paris has always been considered an important city and as such has been well served by airports. From the start of commercial services in 1919 the grass field at Le Bourget was in use for both civil and military movements, but it soon became the airport for Paris. Taken over by the Germans in 1940, Le Bourget derived one distinct benefit from the occupation in the laying of two concrete runways, so when commercial flying recommenced in 1945 the airport could handle the heavier machines developed in the meantime. However, while Le Bourget was perfectly satisfactory for European traffic, the French needed another site for the use of intercontinental movements.

Prewar, a small area of grassland to the south of the capital had been employed by the French Navy as a training school. Known as Orly, it was developed by the Germans during their stay and again two hard runways were laid for the use of the Luftwaffe. At first the latter based bomber units at the airfield, but after a time aircraft production became the main occupation. It soon became apparent to the authorities that Orly was ideally suited for the international airport project, especially since it was also geographically well situated. No time was lost in using Orly for airline traffic after the Liberation and in 1946 work began on a major scheme of expansion.

Due consideration was given to a tangential layout for the runways, but the

system was not adopted. Instead an ambitious scheme for three parallel runways straddling the main Paris-Fontainebleau road was conceived. Nevertheless, by 1949 only a single additional strip had been constructed parallel to one of the pair left by the Germans. In common with many other airports developed in the immediate postwar years, Orly did not enjoy the luxury of permanent buildings, although in appearance and comfort they were far superior to the flimsy accommodation at Heathrow. With the financial state of France creating problems and the growth of air transport being slower than anticipated, Orly's completion became more of a very long-term project.

After a series of prolonged arguments, in 1957 work was at last started on the much delayed programme, leading to the formal opening of Europe's newest terminal building by President de Gaulle on 24 February 1961. Intended to have a wing projecting from each end of the rectangular structure, only that to the west was operational at this stage, although the second was completed during 1962 and, like the first, was equipped with assembly lounges at each of the gates. The general design followed the Paris Airport Authority's precept that an air journey should begin and end at the airport rather than at a city centre terminal. While such an establishment was retained at Les Invalides, it became virtually only a ticket and information office.

Some years later another phase of the expansion plan produced Orly Ouest, a

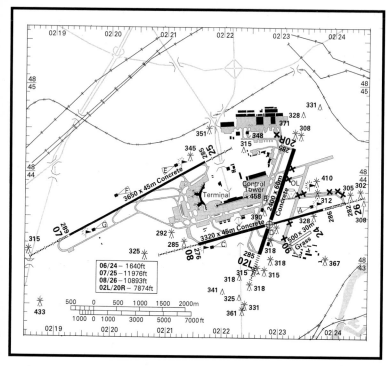

06/24 –	1640ft
07/25 –	11976ft
08/26 –	10893ft
02L/20R –	7874ft

much larger facility than the earlier building, which was now identified as Orly Sud. The newcomer was also equipped with two piers, but these extended at right angles from the front of the main block, airbridges being a standard feature at the dozen or so stands. In the late 1980s there was a strong growth in passenger traffic which called for a substantial capacity increase. To meet partially this demand, the complete refurbishment of Hall 2 at Orly Ouest began so that it will be able to handle the larger wide-bodied types from mid-1990. Work also began on the construction of a new facility designed to accommodate four A330-size aircraft or a combination of six narrow-bodies after its scheduled completion in 1993. A five-level car park directly linked to the terminal was included in the project, while considerable benefit will be derived from the provision of a new transit system to link Orly Ouest and Sud on an elevated track before going underground for the runway crossing.

During 1993 the programme involving

Orly Ouest's new number one terminal unit was completed, producing a capacity increase of some 4 million travellers per year. Work also continued in the number two unit with a scheme which is aimed to reduce congestion and improve security, achieved by separating the flow of incoming and outgoing passengers. Major runway reconstruction work also became operational during the year, which was in time for the influx of new carriers. Previously, Orly had been monopolised by Air Inter's comprehensive domestic network, but in the spring of 1994 the European Commission ordered the French Government to allow more competition following a complaint by TAT and British Airways. After further delays and appeals, it was agreed that limited access would be granted, but that in 1995 only aircraft with a capacity in excess of 200 seats would be permitted.

Location and access: Situated 9 miles (14km) south of Paris. Using Line B of the

RER, the rail service from the city centre takes 25min to reach the airport. RATP bus route 215 from the city centre (Denfert-Rochereau) takes 25min to make the trip.
Terminals: Both buildings have a full range of refreshment areas and shops with a useful supermarket in the basement of Orly Sud. The significance of this is apparent when comparing its prices with those elsewhere in the building.

Spectator facilities: The roof terrace on the Sud terminal is normally open and gives a good view of the activity. Although glass-fronted, the vantage point is suitable for photography with care, bearing in mind the reflections and the southerly aspect. The facility may be closed without warning in the event of security alerts. There are reasonable spots within the building which can be kept for viewing and photography. Outside, several other vantage points can be found, particularly near to the VIP area. Here, aircraft on their way to Runway 25 pass very close to the fence, giving good opportunities for shots with different backgrounds. Whichever spot is chosen there is always the chance that the gendarmerie is opposed to the idea. While these officials generally tolerate the strange pursuits of English-speaking visitors, sometimes local happenings necessitate a tightening of security, especially when VIPs are due. At such times the number of official vehicles and their contents quickly multiplies and it is wise to withdraw without delay.

Operators: Adria Airways (DC-9), AeroMexico (Boeing 767), Aigle Azur (SAAB SF340), Air Algerie (Airbus A310, Boeing 727/737/767), Air Atlantique (ATR-42), Air France (Airbus A300, Boeing 737/747), Air Inter (Airbus A300/320/321/330, Fokker 100), Air Liberte (Airbus A300/310, MD80), Air Littoral (Brasilia, ATR-42, Canadair Regional Jet), Air Malta (Airbus A320, Boeing 737), Air Portugal (Airbus A310/320, Boeing 737), American Airlines (Boeing 767), Aviaco (DC-9, MD80), Balkan (Boeing 737), Bangladesh Biman (DC-10), British Airways (Boeing 767, Fokker 100), Continental Airlines (DC-10), Croatia Airlines (Boeing 737), Cubana (DC-10), Delta Air Lines (Airbus A310, Boeing 767), EAS Europe Airlines (Boeing 727/737), EgyptAir (Airbus A300/320, Boeing 747), Hex Air (Jetstream 31), Iberia (MD80), Icelandair (Boeing 737), IOM French Airlines (DC-10), Iran Air (Boeing 747), Istanbul Airlines (Boeing 737), Middle East Airlines (Airbus A310, Boeing 747), Olympic Airways (Boeing 737), Pakistan International (Airbus A310, Boeing 747), Pulse Aviation (Metro), Regional Airlines (Jetstream 31), Royal Air Maroc (Boeing 727/737/757), Royal Nepal Airlines (Airbus A310), SAR Avions Taxis (Super King Air, Metro), South African Airways (Boeing 747), Tarom (One-Eleven), TAT (Fellowship, Beech 1900, Fokker 100, ATR-42/72), Tower Air (Boeing 747), Tunis Air (Airbus A320, Boeing 727/737), Turkish Airlines (Airbus A340, Boeing 737), USAir (Boeing 767), Viasa (DC-10), Viva Air (Boeing 737).

Movements (1993): Total 204,552. Total passengers 25,368.000.

Runways: 07/25 (11,976ft/3,650m), 08/26 (10,893ft/3,320m), 02L/20R (7,874ft/2,400m), 06/24 (1,640ft/500m — grass).

Radio frequencies: 118.7MHz, 121.05MHz (Tower), 120.85MHz (Approach), 127.75MHz (Departure), 121.7MHz (Ground).

Telephone: (1) 49 75 52 52

Operated by: Aéroports de Paris

Rome (Leonardo da Vinci/Fiumicino)

Officially named Leonardo da Vinci, Rome's international airport opened for business on 16 January 1961, replacing Ciampino in the process. Designed by the Italian Ministry of Air Defence, the airport was actually built by the Ministry of Public Works on a large area of flat ground eminently suitable for future expansion when required. Unusually for the time, the national carrier, Alitalia, was invited to join in the planning stages of the new terminal block, which therefore received the benefit of the airline's practical experience.

Initially, the new airport covered about 250 acres to accommodate two runways, international and domestic terminals and a freight centre. In its first year of service some 2,246,000 passengers used the facility, a total which grew throughout the decade. Eventually in the mid-1970s it became necessary to lengthen the main runway and to construct a new building to be used for domestic operations.

Meanwhile, as a result of an Act of Parliament which became law on 10 November 1973, a new company had been set up to control the running of Leonardo da Vinci and the civilian activities at Ciampino. Known as Aeroporti di Roma SpA, it formally took over the responsibility from the

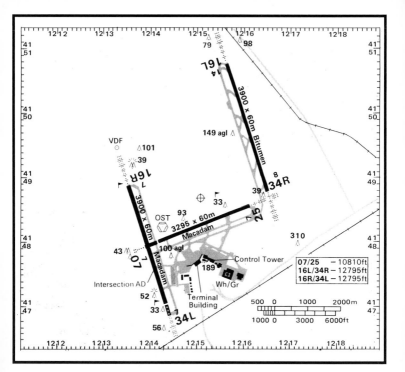

State on 1 July 1974. Under the agreement, almost all airport services that had previously been managed by a number of small contractors were transferred to the new organisation.

A third runway was brought into use in August 1973 and by the end of that year the number of passengers handled annually had risen to 9,705,000, a figure still within the capacity of the airport, which was then the fourth busiest in Europe. To keep ahead of the steady growth, a master plan was produced by the authorities in the 1980s aimed at catering for up to 30 million passengers by the year 2005. Once again Alitalia was actively involved because in 1983 it became a majority shareholder in Aeroporti di Roma.

This latest project, which was conceived with the assistance of an American airport and aeronautical engineering consultancy, will be carried out in stages to prevent any significant disruption of normal activities. In due course a massive new international and domestic terminal covering 300,000sq m is to be constructed, a considerable increase in size over the 90,000sq m area currently in use. In conjunction with this development, 50 airbridges will be installed together with another 25 stands for aircraft, most of them clustered around two additional piers. The first of the latter was earmarked for use by domestic traffic when completed, in this case adding 14 airbridges to the total available. However, it will be the late 1990s before the international section enters service, together with another nine gates. In addition to this expansion, two satellites will be built on the north side to be situated in the centre of the present aircraft parking area. Connected to the main buildings by both overhead and underground walkways, travelators will be necessary in view of the increased distances involved.

Until recently Aeroporti di Roma has financed all of the improvement programmes with the dual purpose of both enhancing the appearance of the concourse and restaurant areas in the international terminal and at the same time ensuring that efficiency is maintained at a high level. With the enormous cost of the latest project, the company will in fact only be responsible for about one third of the initial phase.

Location and access: Situated 16 miles (26km) southwest of the city. Non-stop trains run from Roma Ostiense via Roma Trastevere to the airport station every 30min or so throughout the day between 05.40hrs and 23.30hrs. Journey time is about 25min.

Terminals: A pair of two-storey buildings handle international and domestic passengers, both terminals containing the usual facilities. A sufficient number of restaurants and snack-bars exists to satisfy most hunger pangs, although the cost is likely to induce a sudden loss of appetite.

Spectator facilities: In the early days there was an excellent viewing terrace along the front of both terminals and on the roof of the connecting passageway. These are now but a memory, since the facilities were closed some years ago following the antics of various terrorist groups. There are now few vantage points in the terminal area other than through the windows of the first floor restaurants, or at the domestic end of the new travelator system. Photography is not to be recommended because the police appear to outnumber passengers and are not kindly disposed towards aviation enthusiasts. In the absence of any suitable spots, the perimeter is the only alternative. To the west of the airport, Runway 16R/34L runs parallel to a minor road signposted to Focene and Fregene from the village of Fiumicino. Along this stretch an area of waste ground on the western side provides a convenient car park from which to view the various movements, although much depends upon the wind direction as to the usefulness of the spot. At least there is a reasonable cafe nearby from which to obtain occasional refreshments at sensible prices.

Operators: Adria Airways (Dash Seven), Aeroflot (Airbus A310, IL-86), Aerolineas Argentinas (Boeing 747), AeroMexico (Boeing 767), Aer Lingus (Boeing 737), African International (DC-8), Air Afrique (Airbus A310, DC-10), Air Algerie (Boeing 727), Air China (Boeing 747), Air France (Airbus A320, Boeing 737, Brasilia), Air Gabon (Boeing 747), Air India (Airbus A310), Air Lanka (TriStar), Air Littoral (Brasilia, ATR-42), Air Malta (Boeing 737), Air Mauritius (Boeing 747), Air New Zealand (Boeing 747), Air Portugal (Airbus A320, Boeing 737), Air Seychelles (Boeing 767), Alitalia (Airbus A300/321, Boeing 747, DC-9, MD80/11, ATR-42), ATI (DC-9, MD80), Balkan (Boeing 737), British Airways (Fokker 100, Boeing 737/757/767, Fellowship), Cameroon Airlines (Boeing 747), Canadian Airlines (Boeing 767), Cathay Pacific (Boeing 747), Corse Mediterranée (ATR-42), Croatia Airlines (Boeing 737), Crossair (SAAB SF340/2000), Cyprus Airways (Airbus A320, One-Eleven), Delta Air Lines (Airbus A310, Boeing 767, TriStar), EgyptAir (Airbus A300/320, Boeing 737/767), El Al (Boeing 737/747/757/767), Ethiopian Airlines (Boeing 757/767), Ghana Airways (DC-10), Gulf Air (Boeing 767), Finnair (DC-9, MD80), Garuda (Boeing 747, MD11), Iberia (MD80), Iran Air (Boeing 747), Japan Airlines (Boeing 747), Kenya Airways (Airbus A310), KLM (Boeing 737), Korean Air (Boeing 747), Kuwait Airways (Airbus A300/310), Linhas Aereas de Moçambique (Boeing 767), LOT Polish Airlines (Boeing 737), Lufthansa (Airbus A320, Boeing 737, Canadair Regional Jet, Dash Eight), Luxair (Boeing 737), Malev (Boeing 737/767, Tu-154), Meridiana (MD80), Middle East Airlines (Airbus A310, Boeing 707), Nigeria Airways (Airbus A310), Olympic Airways (Airbus A300, Boeing 737), Pakistan International (Airbus A310), Philippine Airlines (Boeing 747), Qantas (Boeing 747), Royal Air Maroc (Boeing 727/737), Royal Jordanian (Airbus A310/320, Boeing 727), SABENA (Boeing 737), SAS (DC-9, MD80), Saudia (TriStar), Singapore Airlines (Boeing 747), South East European (Fokker 50), Sudan Airways (Airbus A320), Swissair (MD80, Fokker 100), Syrian Arab (Caravelle, Boeing 727), TAAG Angola Airlines (TriStar), Tarom (One-Eleven), Thai Airways International (Boeing 747), Trans World (Boeing 747/767), Tunis Air (Airbus A320, Boeing 727/737), Turkish Airlines (Boeing 737), United Airlines (Boeing 747/767), Varig (Boeing 747/767), Viasa (DC-10).

Only scheduled services operate into Fiumicino, all charter flights using the older Ciampino airport except for emergency diversions.

Movements (1993): Total 220,290. Total passengers 19,851,881.

Runways: 16L/34R (12,795ft/3,900m), 16R/34L (12,795ft/3,900m), 07/25 (10,810ft/3,295m).

Radio frequencies: 118.7MHz, 119.3MHz (Tower), 119.2MHz (Approach), 121.9MHz (Ground).

Telephone: (06) 6595 1.

Operated by: Aeroporti di Roma SpA.

Stockholm (Arlanda)

Prior to the opening of Arlanda the Swedish capital had been served by the conveniently situated Bromma airport, only five miles from the city. However, as early as 1946 it had been recognised by the government that something larger would be required for the anticipated rapid growth in air transport. After due consideration it was decided to build a major new facility at Halmsjon, some 25 miles from Stockholm and initially intended to take over the international traffic. Clearance work was quickly started on the site, which was located in an area covered by a vast forest in the Uppland countryside, but after a relatively short time the project was suspended in 1948. Traffic had not reached the proportions forecast by the authorities, therefore it was concluded that Bromma would be able to cope for many years to come.

After a four-year break, construction was restarted in 1952, but this time the scheme was intended to proceed in stages at a more leisurely pace, the first step being the provision of a concrete runway. Costs had escalated in the intervening period, a factor which resulted in the contractors severely overspending on the budget. In an attempt to solve this problem, it was decided to reduce the quality of the runway to the absolute minimum, but of course this solution was hardly sensible. It meant that when completed in 1954 the strip was so bad that pilots refused to land on it. With the financial limits imposed, little attempt had been made to level the ground, so the undulating runway rose and fell some 9m along its length. In addition, at the eastern end of the 60m-wide expanse of concrete there was a difference of 0.9m in height between the two sides. Scarcely a good start for an international airport.

Nevertheless, despite the high level of criticism, the government decided to continue with the Halmsjon site, although not until after alternatives at Malaroarna and Jordbro had been investigated. Another three years had passed when the go-ahead was given in October 1957, hopefully to bring completion of the first phase in 1960

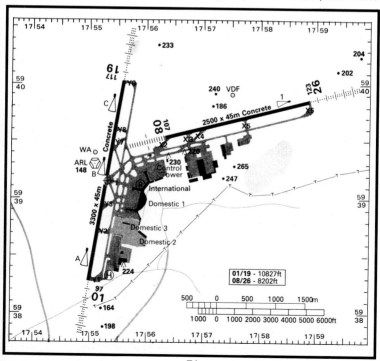

01/19 - 10827ft
08/26 - 8202ft

to allow at least some of the traffic to transfer from Bromma, where noise problems were becoming intolerable. Well before this event it was apparent that the name 'Halmsjon' was not particularly suitable because only Swedes would be able to pronounce it correctly. Something that international travellers could handle was therefore desirable so a contest was held to find a candidate. Half a dozen proposals were awarded prizes, but it was the Place-name Commission which had the task of making the final short-list. After exhaustive discussions both Lunda and Arlanda were proposed and on 9 May 1958 the King-in-Council decreed that the latter would be used in future.

With phase one completed as planned, it was possible to commence commercial operations at the new airport in 1960. On 26 June a short ceremony was held to mark the departure of the inaugural flight to New York by an SAS DC-8, but it was to be another two years before Arlanda was officially opened by His Majesty the King. By now it handled all scheduled international movements, to which were added charters in 1968 and domestic jet-powered aircraft a year later. With this influx the original single terminal quickly became inadequate, so plans were made to provide a separate building for domestic passengers with temporary relief given by the erection of tented accommodation. Charter flights were also rapidly increasing in number, so another terminal was opened in 1972 to handle this business. That same year authorisation was given for a brand-new structure capable of absorbing all international traffic, both scheduled and charter, a role it assumed in 1976.

Next it was the turn of the domestic operators to acquire new premises, an event which took place on 1 October 1983, thereby allowing the removal of the earlier building. Such a fate did not await the charter terminal when it ceased to be used for its intended purpose. Instead this was converted into a freight centre in 1985 for the growing number of cargo aircraft using Arlanda. As an interim measure, the building had been used enterprisingly to house an exhibition of historic and vintage aircraft which have all now been rehoused in a Space and Aviation Museum within the airport.

During its first 25 years, Arlanda has been steadily expanded, the latest development including plans for a third runway, and the domestic terminal, which

opened in October 1989. It is also envisaged that another pier will be necessary for international use by the turn of the century, and that at some time in the future a fourth runway will be laid. Access roads to the airport are to be improved in view of the volume of passengers attempting the journey from Stockholm, and a rail link with the city is receiving active consideration — a development first mooted as long ago as 1963.

Location and access: Situated 25 miles (40km) northwest of Stockholm. There is a frequent SL City Line bus service from the central railway station which takes 45min for the journey. SL West suburban line runs from the city centre via a number of points connecting with the underground system. This trip takes 50min.

Terminals: Separate interconnected buildings for international and domestic use with two and one piers respectively. Airbridge loading is carried out on all three. All the necessary refreshment facilities are contained in both terminals with a fine array of shops located in Pier A of the international building. Arlanda Centre is a complex located between the two terminals and is intended to improve the service to passengers by providing yet more shops and other facilities.

Spectator facilities: The observation terrace was closed several years ago, a fate shared by a small, shortlived replacement enclosure. There appears little likelihood of the facilities being reopened since the authority has removed all signs relating to the area. A window seat in the international terminal's cafe offers a view of parts of the apron, but is less than ideal. The end of the pier offers good views of all movements. Many of the more interesting commuter movements are not visible, while the international traffic involves carriers to be seen in far better conditions at other airports. Landing shots are possible from vantage points near the ends of runways 01 and 26.

Operators: Aeroflot (Tu-154, IL-62), Air Algerie (Boeing 737), Air Express (Super King Air), Air France (Boeing 737), Air Nordic Sweden (Friendship), Air Portugal (Boeing 737), Airborne of Sweden (Titan), Alitalia (DC-9, MD80), American Airlines (Boeing 767), Austrian Airlines (MD80), Balkan (Boeing 737, Tu-154), British Airways (Boeing 737/757, Fokker 100), CSA Czechoslovak Airlines (Tu-134), Delta Air Lines (Airbus A310, Boeing 767), Deutsche

BA (Boeing 737), EgyptAir (Airbus A320), El Al (Boeing 757), Falcon Aviation (Boeing 737), Finnair (DC-9, MD80, ATR-72), Flying Enterprise (Metro, Short SD3-30), Holmstroem Air (Dornier Do228, Short SD3-60), Iberia (Airbus A320, MD80), Icelandair (Boeing 737/757), Kenya Airways (Airbus A310), KLM (Boeing 737, Fokker 100), Latavio Latvian Airlines (Boeing 737), Lauda Air (Canadair Regional Jet), Lithuanian Airlines (Boeing 737), LOT Polish Airlines (Boeing 737), Lufthansa (Boeing 737, Fokker 50, Canadair Regional Jet), Maersk Air (Fokker 50), Malev (Boeing 737), Nyge-Aero (Bandeirante), Olympic Airways (Boeing 737), SABENA (Boeing 737), SAS (DC-9, MD80, Boeing 737/767, Fellowship), Skyways (SAAB SF340), Swissair (MD80), Tarom (One-Eleven), Thai Airways International (Boeing 747), Transwede (Fokker 100, MD80), Turkish Airlines (Boeing 737), West Air Sweden (Super King Air, Westwind).

Movements (1993): Total 221,900. Total passengers 12,466,000.

Runways: 01L/19R (10,827ft/3,300m), 08/26 (8,202ft/2,500m). A new 10,000ft runway will become 01R/19L later in the 1990s, while a fourth strip is part of the long-term strategy.

Radio frequencies: 118.5MHz, 125.125MHz (Tower), 120.5MHz, 123.3MHz (Approach).

Telephone: (08) 797 6100

Operated by: Board of Civil Aviation

Vienna (Schwechat)

Austria was one of the first European countries to sustain regular air transport services, but it was just a year or so before the start of World War 2 that construction began on the site of Vienna's new airport, located between the villages of Fischamend and Schwechat. By this time Germany had taken control of the country's affairs, including the merging of the national carrier with Lufthansa. Very little civil flying continued during the war, especially when the shortlived airport came under the control of the Heinkel organisation. Thereafter the base was used for flight testing many of the advanced prototypes conceived by the company, necessitating the laying of a 4,921ft (1,500m) hard runway. This later became the target for the Allied air forces on a number of occasions, resulting in serious damage being inflicted. With Germany defeated, the airport underwent a period of essential repair work before it could be used by the occupying forces.

Civil traffic was permitted to restart in 1946 on a small scale, but it was not until 1953 that much growth was apparent, growth coincidental with the formation of the Vienna Airport Authority. One of the latter's first decisions was to increase the length of the runway, followed by the design and construction of a new terminal. Even in the late 1950s the somewhat basic temporary arrangements were still in use for handling passengers. A fairly orthodox design was adopted for the building although, in the light of experience and airline requirements, this now incorporates an eight-gate pier at its eastern end. When completed in 1988 it introduced the airport to airbridge loading, superseding to some extent the use of the traditional bus from terminal to aircraft. Some years earlier the single runway was deemed incapable of handling the traffic, so approval was sought to construct another strip. This was duly received and eventually 16/34 came into use on 6 October 1977.

Cargo work has also increased considerably at Vienna in recent years, which encouraged the provision of a new freight centre in 1986. Several airlines now operate freight-only flights with 747s while others employ combi versions on their normal passenger routes.

Austria is, of course, well known for its abundance of snow. Whereas this pleases those wishing to slide down hills, its presence on the airport is not so welcome. Coupled with the high winds often experienced locally, the ground services are fully occupied in keeping Schwechat open during the winter months. At least the arrival of the white precipitation does not come as a surprise to the well trained staff operating the fleet of snow ploughs and blowers.

Location and access: Situated 11 miles (18km) southeast of Vienna. A motorway passes nearby from which there is an access spur. An hourly OBB rail service links the city centre stations (Wien Nord and Wien Mitte) directly with the airport, taking 30min for the journey. By OBB bus from the centre (Hilton Hotel) or from Wien South station the trip takes 20min, while from Wien West another 15min has to be added.

Terminal: The large multi-storey building has acquired an impressive new arrivals hall. Although the usual restaurants, bars and shops exist within the main block, the new

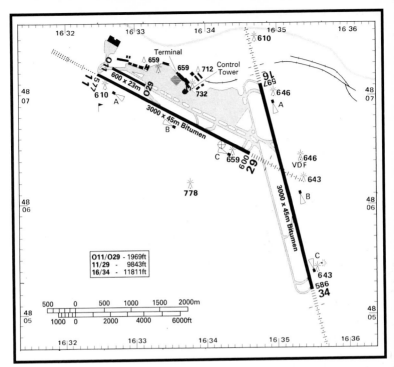

pier contains eight holding lounges each with its own security facility. Not a particularly new idea, nevertheless it was adopted by the Vienna authorities in accordance with the airline's wishes to speed the movement of passengers with greater security.

Spectator facilities: A roof terrace overlooking some of the apron is provided at the western end of the terminal, which also has several museum exhibits on display. These change from time to time as they are moved to sites elsewhere. In common with many other airports, the building faces south, which does not help photography in the middle of the day. The lounge area on the top floor offers good views of the apron and runway, but photography is not possible due to the double-glazed windows. Outside, to the right of the terminal building and beyond the cargo facility, lies the general aviation area. This is very close to the taxiway and offers the opportunity for shots of passing traffic. The multi-storey car parks outside the

terminal provide different vantage points, with views of the apron and Runway 34 that are not visible from the roof. However, the local security staff do not tolerate stationary pedestrians so it is wise to forgo a visit to these buildings.

Operators: Adria Airways (Dash Seven), Aeroflot (Tu-154), Air Algerie (Boeing 727/737), Air China (Boeing 767), Air Engiadina (Dornier 328), Air Malta (Boeing 737), Air Portugal (Boeing 737), Albanian Airlines (Dash Eight), Alitalia (MD80), Austrian Airlines (Airbus A310, MD80), Austrian Air Services (Dash Eight, Fokker 50), Balkan (Airbus A320), Belavia (Tu-134), British Airways (Boeing 737/757), Croatia Airlines (ATR-42), CSA Czechoslovak Airlines (LET 410, ATR-72), Cyprus Airways (Airbus A320), Delta Air Lines (Airbus A310, Boeing 727/767, TriStar), EgyptAir (Airbus A320), El Al (Boeing 737/757), Eurowings (ATR-42), EVA Airways (Boeing 747), Finnair (MD80), Garuda (Boeing 747), Icelandair (Boeing 737), Istanbul Airlines (Boeing 737), KLM (Boeing 737), Latavio Latvian Airlines

(Tu-134), Lauda Air (Boeing 737/767, Canadair Regional Jet), LOT Polish Airlines (Boeing 737), Lufthansa (Airbus A320, Boeing 737, Fokker 50, Dash Eight, Canadair Regional Jet), Luxair (Brasilia), Malaysian Airlines (Boeing 747), Malev (Tu-134, Yak-40), Olympic Airways (Boeing 737), Rheintalflug (Dash Eight), Royal Jordanian (Airbus A320), SABENA (Boeing 737), SAS (MD80), Singapore Airlines (Boeing 747), Tarom (One-Eleven), Trans World (Boeing 767), Tunis Air (Airbus A320,

Boeing 737), Tyrolean Airways (Dash Eight), Turkish Airlines (BAe 146, Boeing 737, DC-9), Ukraine International (Boeing 737).
Movements (1993): Total 117,300. Total passengers 7,006,000.
Runways: 16/34 (11,811ft/3,600m), 11/29 (9,843ft/3,000m).
Radio frequencies: 118.725MHz, 121.2MHz (Tower), 119.8MHz, 124.55MHz, 128.2MHz (Radar), 121.6MHz (Ground).
Telephone: (1) 711 100
Operated by: Vienna Airport Authority

Zürich (Kloten)

Surprisingly, Zürich's international airport at Kloten handles over 13 million passengers annually, a total about 12 times greater than the entire population of the city plus its environs. Of course its important business community generates a good proportion of the traffic, but its role as a gateway for much of Switzerland plus the southern areas of both Germany and Austria has swollen the numbers considerably. It is also actively marketed as a hub for intercontinental

services, which has resulted in travellers being ferried in for their long-haul flights from many other airports in Europe.

Of postwar construction, work on Kloten began in the summer of 1946, leading to the completion of the first runway in June 1948, followed by the main instrument landing strip in November of the same year. At this stage it was possible to transfer all commercial traffic from its previous base at the nearby military airfield of Dubendorf. Nevertheless, it was not until mid-1953 that the new airport was completed and ready

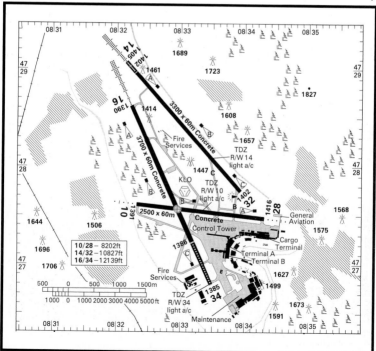

for its official opening on 29 August.

This event was also a turning point in Swiss aviation generally, which quickly indicated to the authorities that their newly created facility was already inadequate. Plans were drawn up for a comprehensive expansion programme including the lengthening of the runways and the provision of more parking stands for the aircraft. Unfortunately, the scheme was rejected following a referendum held for the citizens by the Canton of Zürich. They had already financed the original project and were unwilling to invest yet more millions in the latest proposal. A revised plan of more modest proportions was submitted for approval in the following year, and this received the go-ahead. Runway extensions were still included, but they were not taken to the lengths originally specified. Other building work carried out involved various administrative accommodations and the erection of a large hangar capable of housing 747s.

Even before the completion of this second phase, further expansion gained approval without delay. This time the principal improvement was the provision of a third runway for instrument approaches. A greatly increased area of apron was laid to help ease congestion on the ground, but probably the most important feature was the construction of Terminal B complete with pier and loading bridges. The latter facility was subsequently added to Terminal A enabling it to handle between 13 and 18 airliners, depending on type. After its reopening it was devoted exclusively to all European flights plus those of Pan Am and TWA. All intercontinental and charter operations thereafter became the responsibility of Terminal B. With traffic well within the capacity of the existing runway system, it is very unlikely that a fourth will be laid. This is fortunate because any suggestion of such a development would be decidedly unpopular with the local population.

Access was greatly improved in 1980 when Swiss Federal Railways connected the airport with its extensive network by integrating it into the main east-west line. Five trains per hour run to and from the city to play a major part in making this mode of transport increasingly popular with passengers and visitors. During its first year of operation the trains carried 3.9 million people, a total that continues to show a healthy annual increase. Located two floors below street level, the station is connected to both terminals either by bridge or tunnel. Passengers using this facility now have the opportunity to check-in luggage at any of 100 Swiss rail stations plus some of the postal coach points. The bags are then conveyed to the final destination to await pickup.

Kloten's impact on the district's economy is considerable, providing employment for some 16,000 people, of whom 10,000 are with Swissair. A large number of important companies depend on the fast import and export of their goods to survive. Air freight movements have

Above: The pier on the left of the picture accommodates Zürich's rooftop viewing area.
Kloten Airport Authority

therefore increased steadily because it is a method of transportation favoured by those concerned with watches, clocks and delicate scientific instruments. Zürich serves about 60% of the total Swiss territory, with most of the remainder dependent on Geneva.

Early in the 1990s it became apparent that some form of expansion would eventually become necessary in order to cope with the steadily increasing number of passengers using Kloten each year. Outline plans were therefore drawn up for the construction of aircraft stands in the area between the three runways. Parking positions for about 30 machines will be provided, together with an island pier complete with passenger gates. Following the necessary alterations to the taxiway system, the new zone will be an ideal position for arriving and departing aircraft with much reduced ground distances involved. A tunnel will have to be built for passenger access to the midfield location, no doubt with some form of transportation in view of the long distance from the main terminal buildings, which will still be used for check-in arrangements. Up to 80 counters for the latter procedure will also be installed in the railway station for the greater convenience of those using train services. The entire project is estimated to require an investment of some SFr2 billion, shared in varying amounts by the airport's partners. Work is not expected to start until the end of the decade, with completion of the entire undertaking within ten years.

Location and access: Situated 7.5 miles (12km) north of Zürich. Direct motorway link with the city and other routes. When parking, the signs indicating 'Zuschauer' should be followed. Regular trains take 11min for the journey between the main railway station and the airport. The latter is also reached directly from a number of other locations. The Verkehrsbetriebe Winterthur bus service links the city centre bus station with the airport. Journey time is 40min.

Spectator facilities: An excellent observation deck is provided on the roof of Terminal B's pier, entry to which can be gained on payment of a small fee. A strict security check is imposed with lockers provided for the safe keeping of unacceptable items. Refreshment facilities of a high standard are available on the deck which, although expensive, are extremely welcome on hot days. The area provides an

excellent vantage point for photography, especially of the long-haul types. Since the reconstruction of Terminal A it is more difficult to follow the movements on the far side of the building, but this problem can by overcome by moving to multi-storey car park F. This vantage point offers excellent views and opportunities for photographs, although a 300mm zoom lens is really necessary. Due to the lack of walls, structures of this type are not noted for their draught-free comfort, so such premises in Switzerland can be expected to be chilly. As a bonus, the airport offers regular airport tours by bus starting from the observation deck. These are well worth the cost as during the course of the journey it is possible to secure photographs that would be impossible from other spots. Towards the end of the trip the bus visits a small fenced enclosure near to the intersection of runways 10/28 and 16/34. While luck plays a part, several movements will usually occur while you are out of the vehicle. For those with transport, there are numerous locations around the perimeter which provide a change of scene, those particularly useful being near the thresholds of runways 10, 14 and 28. There is a car park complete with a coffee bar at the end of Runway 14.

Operators: Adria Airways (DC-9, Dash Seven), Aer Lingus (Boeing 737), Aeroflot (Tu-154), Aero Jet (BAe 146), Aero Lloyd (MD80), Aerolineas Argentinas (Boeing 747), African Safari (DC-10), Air Afrique (Airbus A310), Air Algerie (Boeing 737/757), Air Canada (Boeing 767), Air China (Boeing 747), Air Columbus (Boeing 737), Air Dolomiti (ATR-42, Dash Eight), Air Engiadina (Jetstream 31), Air Europa (Boeing 737/757), Air France (Airbus A320, Boeing 737, Fellowship), Air Holland (Boeing 757), Air Lanka (TriStar), Air Madagascar (Boeing 747), Air Malta (Boeing 737), Air Mauritius (Boeing 747/767), Air Portugal (Airbus A320, Boeing 737), Air Provence (Gulfstream 1), Air Seychelles (Boeing 767), Alitalia (MD80, DC-9), Air 2000 (Boeing 757), American Airlines (Boeing 767), Arkia (Boeing 757), ATI (MD80), Austrian Airlines (Dash Eight), Balair CTA (Airbus A310, MD80), Balkan (Boeing 737), Belavia (Tu-134), Britannia Airways (Boeing 757/767), British Airways (Airbus A320, Boeing 737/757), BWIA International (TriStar), Caledonian Airways (Airbus A320, Boeing 757, TriStar), Cathay Pacific (Boeing 747), Centennial (MD80), Classic Air (DC-3), Corse Mediterranée (ATR-42), Croatia Airlines (Boeing 737), Crossair (SAAB SF340/2000, Fokker 50,

BAe 146, Avro RJ85), CSA Czechoslovak Airlines (ATR-72, Boeing 737, Tu-134/154), Delta Air Lines (Airbus A310, Boeing 747/767, MD11), Cyprus Airways (Airbus A310/320), Deutsche BA (SAAB SF340), EgyptAir (Airbus A310/320, Boeing 737/767), El Al (Boeing 747/757), Emirates (Airbus A300/310), Eurocypria (Airbus A320), Eurofly (DC-9), Eurowings (ATR-42), Finnair (MD80), Futura (Boeing 737), Garuda (Boeing 747, MD11), GB Airways (Boeing 737), Gulf Air (Boeing 767), Iberia (MD80), Icelandair (Boeing 737/757), Istanbul Airlines (Boeing 727/737), Japan Airlines (Boeing 747), Kenya Airways (Airbus A310), KLM (Boeing 737, Fokker 100), Korean Air (Boeing 747, MD11), LOT Polish Airlines (Boeing 737), LTE (Boeing 757), Lufthansa (Airbus A320, Boeing 737, Fokker 50, Canadair Regional Jet), Maersk Air (Boeing 737), Malaysian Airlines (Boeing 747), Malev (Boeing 737), Meridiana (DC-9, MD80), Middle East Airlines (Airbus A310), Monarch Airlines (Boeing 757), Oasis (MD80), Olympic Airways (Boeing 737), Onur Air (Airbus A320), Pegasus (Boeing 737), Portugalia (Fokker 100), Royal Air Maroc (Boeing 727/737), Royal Brunei Airlines (Boeing 767), SABENA (Boeing 737), SAS (MD80), Singapore Airlines (Boeing 747), Sobelair (Boeing 737), South African Airways (Boeing 747), Swissair (Airbus A310, Boeing 747, Fokker 100, MD80/11), Tarom (One-Eleven), Tatra Air (SAAB SF340), TEA Switzerland (Boeing 737), Thai Airways International (MD11), Trans World (Boeing 747/767), Transaero (Boeing 737), Tunis Air (Airbus A320, Boeing 727/737), Turkish Airlines (Airbus A310, Boeing 737), Ukraine International (Boeing 737), United Airlines (Boeing 747/767), Varig (MD11), Viasa (DC-10), Viva Air (Boeing 737), ZAS Airline of Egypt.

Movements (1993): Total 233,884. Total passengers 13,574,085.
Runways: 16/34 (12,139ft/3,700m), 14/32 (10,827ft/3,300m), 10/28 (8,202ft/2,500m).
Radio frequencies: 118.1MHz, 127.75MHz (Tower), 121.8MHz (Approach), 125.95MHz (Departure), 121.9MHz 119.7MHz (Ground).
Telephone: (01) 816 2211
Operated by: Zürich Airport Authority

Part 2 — Other Airports

Austria
Innsbruck

The airport is located 3.5 miles (5.5km) west of the city and is reached by using the A12 motorway or road 171. Although built in the River Inn valley, the site is still 1,906ft/581m above sea level and is surrounded by a fine selection of hills and mountains. These were responsible for the loss of an inbound British Eagle Britannia in February 1964, an incident which generated a lot of adverse publicity. Nowadays Innsbruck is the home of Tyrolean Airways, which operates schedules and charters with its Dash Eight fleet and remaining Dash Sevens. Other operators include Crossair, using SAAB 340s, and Air UK, the latter flying schedules from Stansted with BAe 146s. During the winter of 1992-3 Air UK Leisure began a series of ski charters into the airport with a Boeing 737-400, a type also employed by Lauda Air. Special training is necessary for crews employed on the services. Good views of the activity can be obtained from the balcony along the front of the terminal building, access being via a café where prices discourage a lengthy stay. A reasonable number of light and general aviation types are usually to be seen around the apron area.
(Runway 08/26 (6,561ft/2,000m);
Tower 120.1MHz/Approach 118.95MHz)

Salzburg

Situated 3 miles (5km) west-southwest of the city, this airport provides a convenient gateway to the Alpine holiday areas. As a result, charter traffic is quite numerous, while scheduled movements are mainly by airlines linking the city to Germany and Switzerland, with only a small number serving other destinations. Carriers likely to be noted are Lufthansa (Boeing 737), Swissair (MD80), Austrian Airlines (MD80), Air France (Boeing 737) and Tyrolean/Austrian (Fokker 50). Charter flights include those operated by Condor (Boeing 757/767), Hapag-Lloyd (Boeing 737, Airbus A310), Braathens (Boeing 737) and Lauda Air (Boeing 737). A roof terrace was provided when the terminal was built, but the modern trend to charge an entrance fee has reduced its appeal,

especially since views are now more restricted than in the past. However, at least it has remained open, with access via a turnstyle which only digests coins to the value of 5sch. (Runway 16/34 (9,350ft/2,850m);
Tower 118.1MHz/Approach 123.725MHz)

Belgium
Antwerp (Deurne)

This fairly quiet airport is conveniently located 2 miles (3km) southeast of the city centre. Its modest passenger accommodation of prewar origin is all located in the southeast corner of the site, but is generally adequate to handle the well-spaced scheduled services. London is the most popular destination for travellers from Deurne, which is linked to Gatwick, Heathrow and London City. There is a good vantage point to the side of the building, although a more substantial fence has been erected to replace its well-holed predecessor. Alternatively, the airport's café has an outside terrace with a similar view, but with the added benefit of offering a chair and refreshment for the weary traveller. Due to the aspect of these spots, the sun can prove a nuisance during the middle hours of the day. Fortunately, Antwerp has an enlightened authority which will readily allow access to the apron and hangars on request. Passports are exchanged for an airside permit for the duration of the tour, which is usually escorted. Airlines seen regularly are CityFlyer with 360s and ATR-42s, SABENA using a Dash Eight leased from Schreiner and the locally-based Fokker 50-equipped VLM. (Runway 11/29 (4,839ft/1,475m);
Tower 121.4MHz/Approach 119.7MHz)

Ostend

Located 3 miles (5km) southwest of the town, this airport possesses a spacious terminal building overlooking a large apron and a runway which would do justice to a major international centre. Yet for much of the time all is serene, the only movement being the control surfaces of an abandoned 707 flapping in the breeze. There are no longer any passenger schedules, so cargo work is now the main source of income for the authorities. This activity is certainly responsible for regular visits by little-known airlines from unfamiliar countries, generally operating 707s or DC-8s in their twilight years. Appearances by eastern European carriers are also on the increase, IL-76s apparently being their favourite equipment.

The airport's excellent position and size are ideal for crew training sorties, so aircraft from airlines such as SABENA are to be seen from time to time. It is also the choice of many private aircraft about to embark on the cross-Channel leg of a trip to Britain. When the terminal was constructed, the planners thoughtfully provided an excellent roof terrace with access via two wide, parallel stairways. Occasionally the climb to the top was worth the effort with the sight of some uncluttered gem resting on the otherwise deserted concrete. Sadly, even this is no longer possible. In their wisdom, the authorities have employed the skills of local bricklayers to build a wall at the bottom of the stairs, thereby preventing any access to the roof except through a door provided for the use of authorised personnel. In the past the restaurant also offered photographic opportunities through the sliding windows, but these have also been changed to render them useless for such a purpose. Fortunately, vantage points exist at both ends of the single runway, but of course only the patient will be rewarded. (Runway 08/26 (10,500ft/3,200m);
Tower 118.7MHz/Approach 120.6MHz)

Canary Islands

Not so long ago the Canaries offered a winter haven for the nobility, but this is no longer the case. During the past 20 years or so the islands have become extremely popular with tourists and now attract year-round traffic from the UK and mainland Europe. Largest and busiest is Tenerife, an island with a contrasting climate between the north and south coasts. The division is marked by Mount Teide, a formidable obstruction some 12,000ft in height. For many years all commercial movements were handled by Los Rodeos airport, located near the capital, Santa Cruz, but after the disastrous runway collision between a pair of 747s in 1977 and several other accidents involving the terrain, the authorities constructed a new airport in the south. Only Binter Canarias' inter-island domestic flights, the occasional Iberia schedule and light aircraft now use Los Rodeos, where limited viewing is possible from the side of the terminal or Aero Club entrance.

Known as Reina Sofia, the replacement site is located in a relatively flat area with approaches to the single runway made over the sea. The terminal building has been extended several times since its initial opening, the latest work including a welcome rearrangement to the check-in facilities, which had previously been less than ideal. There is a roof terrace offering a good vantage point for photography, but unfortunately it is accessible only to departing passengers. Since the building faces south, the sun is not ideally positioned, with early morning or late afternoon offering the best opportunities. Most of the movements are those of charter carriers, including most of the UK airlines, but the combination of bright weather and an unusual background can produce some useful shots. Alternative locations can be found to the west of the terminal, while elsewhere around the perimeter there are a few suitable spots to be found, but all involve a lengthy and strenuous walk. (Runway 08/26; Tower 119.0MHz/Approach 120.3MHz/Ground 121.9MHz, Canarias Control 126.5MHz)

Fuerteventura is the second largest island of the Canaries' group in terms of area, but it possesses the quietest airport of the four main destinations. It was not until the late 1980s that the small and inadequate terminal building was replaced by more suitable premises, but despite the island's growth in popularity, movements are still meagre when compared with its neighbours. Nevertheless, even familiar subjects can become attractive with the addition of a conveniently placed mountain in the background. To reach such a vantage point it is necessary to be on the southern perimeter, a desolate and barren spot usually frequented by a large collection of goats, each animal being equipped with a bell. Rocks and other earthworks left after the completion of the airport provide the necessary height to photograph over the fence. (Runway 01/19; Tower 118.5MHz/Ground 121.7MHz)

The standard rectangular terminal building at Las Palmas was extended in early 1993 to meet the increased traffic demands. The airport's single runway is also used by the resident military units, but the bulk of the movements are provided by charter airlines. Unusually, there is a landside viewing terrace, but this is behind glass and faces into the sun, thereby producing difficult conditions for photographers. A superior terrace was available for those airside, but this has been closed following an extension to the departure lounge. All movements can be seen (but not photographed) through the large windows, so an early check-in is therefore an advantage, although not always possible if committed to a coach transfer. (Runway 03/21;
Tower 118.30MHz/Approach 124.30MHz)

Although Lanzarote is not as busy as its two larger neighbours, the airport provides excellent vantage points for photography, although not in the vicinity of the terminal. With the site stretching parallel to the uncrowded public beach, access is no problem and is within walking distance of the nearby holiday complexes. If accommodated elsewhere a car becomes necessary, but parking is no problem. A good selection of hills and junior mountains appear in the background of all photographs, often crowned by a seemingly immovable piece of cumulus cloud. By 13.00hrs the sun has moved to a less helpful position, but this can be overcome by moving around the end of the runway. Since the prevailing wind tends to be from the north-east, landings are usually over the sea, which conveniently produces a different background from the morning session. The majority of the movements are generated by European charter traffic, but some of the airlines are not particularly common in the UK. Spanish scheduled flights are operated by Iberia, Aviaco and Viva, while Binter Canarias' CN235s and ATRs appear at regular intervals on inter-island sorties. (Runway 04/22; Tower/Approach 120.7MHz, 121.8MHz/Ground 121.8MHz)

Channel Islands
Jersey

Hardly a major European airport, yet it is one of the busiest in the UK on summer Saturdays. A continuous stream of charter and scheduled flights bring the new intake of holidaymakers to the island, the aircraft staying only a short time before taking the return load back to the mainland. The full range of UK airlines is paraded in front of the observer located at the excellent vantage point on the right-hand side of the terminal roof. Many of the British airlines have a share of the market, so during the day most put in an appearance at least once, but it is not impossible to photograph the entire fleet of some carriers. Several European operators now have schedules to the island, while conferences and similar events frequently generate non-scheduled movements. There is a danger that all shots will have the same background, so it is useful to move base to either end of the runway, where equally good vantage points are available. Given good weather, a most enjoyable and profitable day can be spent. Unfortunately, Jersey can be plagued with less than ideal conditions which can change

Top: Binter Canarias operates inter-island services in the Canary group, Fuerteventura being the destination for the ATR-72 EC-FKQ. *AJW*

Below: Good landing shots can be obtained at Lanzarote, where the occasional movement by a military CASA 212 brings some variation to the diet of charter carriers. *AJW*

Top left : Belgian carriers VLM and SABENA operate into Antwerp/Deurne with Fokker 50s and Dash Eights respectively, the latter on lease from Schreiner. *AJW*

Middle left: A varied selection of subjects can be found at Antwerp including types such as the EMB-121A Xingu OO-SXD. *AJW*

Bottom left: EAS Europe Airlines provided 737-300 F-BKTB for this shot from Tenerife's roof terrace. *AJW*

very quickly from warm, dry and sunny to cold, damp and foggy. While Saturday is undoubtedly superior in terms of traffic quality and quantity, Sunday is a good second choice. Weekdays are much quieter, with little to warrant much excitement. (Runway 09/27 (5,597ft/1,706m); Tower 119.45MHz/Approach 125.2MHz, 120.3MHz)

Denmark
Billund

This is now the country's main charter airport and is situated in the middle of Jutland, 1.2 miles (2km) northeast of the city. Used by Danes for holiday flights, Billund also attracts incoming business due to the presence of Legoland next to the terminal. Regular services link the airport with Copenhagen and are flown by Maersk's Boeing 737s and Fokker 50s. All of the Danish charter companies are to be seen, including Sterling European (Boeing 727), Premiair (Airbus A320, DC-10) and Maersk (Boeing 737). (Runway 09/27 (10,170ft/3,100m); Tower 118.5MHz/Approach 119.25MHz)

Esbjerg

Maersk Fokker 50s maintain the relatively few domestic schedules serving this centre, located 5 miles (8km) northeast of the town, on the west coast of Denmark. Since the area is associated with the North Sea oil industry, it was the reason for a number of attempts by airlines to establish a link with Britain. Air UK offered a service for a time, dropping it in due course in favour of Air Ecosse, although this carrier did no better. The Danish carrier Cimber Air then began to serve Humberside with ATR-42s, which soon gave way to the smaller Nord 262. Nowadays it is Business Air which provides the regular link from Aberdeen, with connections to the East Midlands, Edinburgh and Manchester. Loads have steadily increased to justify a daily round trip by a SAAB SF340, a type which replaced the Bandeirante on the schedule. From Esbjerg's terminal all movements can be seen through the glass windows of the buffet, or alternatively there is a fence on either side of the building which offers suitable vantage points. (Runway 08/26 (8,530ft/2,600m); Tower 120.15MHz).

Eire
Shannon

Situated some 11 miles (17.7km) west-northwest of Limerick, prosperity came to Shannon when it was an important refuelling point before non-stop transatlantic crossings became commonplace. With the advent of the longer range jets, traffic steadily declined from 1958 until only a fraction of the movements were recorded. In an attempt to restore the airport's commercial success, the Irish authorities developed it as a major freight centre and a duty-free zone. As had been hoped, it attracted a considerable business boom and even the number of passengers handled began to improve. Scheduled operators include Aer Lingus, Aeroflot and Delta Air Lines, while the airport is frequently used for crew training sessions by a variety of carriers. Passenger traffic has also grown in recent times, with Saturdays traditionally being the busiest day. A considerable amount of overhaul and refurbishing work is carried out, resulting in a good selecion of unusual airline liveries being seen. The viewing area has been closed for some time, although there are good views of the apron from the departure lounge windows once airside. (Runways 06/24 (10,498ft/3,200m, 13/31 (5,642ft/1,720m); Tower 118.8MHz/Approach 121.4MHz, 120.2MHz)

France
Avignon (Caumont)

France has an abundance of regional airports, usually served by a commuter airline twice daily. In this case Air Jet provides the schedules with Friendships to link Avignon, 4 miles (6.5km) southeast of the town, with Lyon morning and evening. Between the spells of activity there is plenty of time to obtain a good photograph. (Runway 17/35 (4,396ft/1,340m); Tower 122.6MHz)

Beauvais (Tille)

No scheduled services visit the airport nowadays, although at one time coach/air operations from the UK were commonplace. Situated 2 miles (3.2km) north-northeast of the town, it is employed mainly by charter carriers, but even these are very infrequent. The excellent roof terrace is wasted at such a quiet spot and is visited by few. (Runways 13/31 (7,972ft/2,430m), 05/23 (3,624ft/1,105m); Tower 121.4MHz/Approach 119.9MHz)

Bordeaux (Merignac)

A busier than usual regional airport situated

some 7 miles (12km) west of the city, Merignac attracts scheduled services by a number of operators including Air Inter (Airbus A300/320/321, Fokker 100), Air France (Boeing 737/747, Airbus A300, Fellowship), Air Afrique (DC-10, Airbus A300), Air Littoral (Brasilia, ATR-42/72), British Airways (Boeing 737/757), TAT (ATR-42) and Tunis Air (Boeing 727/737). A good photographic vantage point is afforded by the spectators' terrace, from which both military and civil movements can be seen with ease. The presence of the Falcon production line also produces items of interest. Certainly a good airport to visit, if only to obtain photographs of Air Inter's fleet with different backgrounds. (Runways 05/23 (10,170ft/3,100m), 11/29 (7,923ft/2,415m);
Tower 118.3MHz/Approach 118.6MHz, 121.2MHz)

Chambéry (Aix-les-Bains)

Easily reached from the Geneva-Grenoble main road, this airport lies 4 miles (6km) northwest of Chambéry and is served by TAT schedules to Paris. Good, uncluttered photographs can be obtained of subjects otherwise familiar elsewhere. (Runway 18/36 (5,806ft/1,770m);
Tower 118.3MHz/Approach 123.7MHz)

Clermont-Ferrand (Aulnat)

Situated 4 miles (6km) east of the town, the airport is linked to a small number of destinations by Air Littoral and Air Inter, the latter flying on the Paris route with A320s. A high roof terrace gives good views and reasonable shots, although a ground level vantage point is preferable. Such a spot can be found along the D54 road where the taxiway and holding point for Runway 27 is helpfully close to the fence. Much therefore depends upon the wind direction. (Runway 09/27 (9,891ft/3,015m); Tower 118.5MHz/Approach 125.00MHz)

Grenoble (St Geoirs)

During the winter sports season, charter flights increase the number of air transport movements from this airport, which lies 24 miles (39km) northwest of Grenoble, although many are of British origin. Schedules are mainly the responsibility of Air Inter on the Paris run. For those wishing to travel to warmer climes, a Nice service is provided by Air Littoral. A ground enclosure alongside the terminal provides an excellent vantage point from which to view the activity. (Runway 09/27 (10,000ft/3,050m); Tower 119.3MHz/Approach 120.4MHz)

Lille (Lesquin)

This is another airport able to offer good views from a roof terrace but not a lot else. Located 9 miles (15km) southeast of the city, its commercial activity is not great, but Air Inter does have a presence at infrequent times during the day. Flandre Air offers links with Metz and Rennes on weekdays with connections to Nice and Brest, but the periods of operation follow the French traditional holiday breaks. (Runways 02/20 (4,265ft/1,300m), 08/26 (9,268ft/2,825m); Tower 118.35MHz/Approach 127.9MHz)

Lyon (Satolas)

Scheduled traffic serving the airport, located 15.5 miles (25km) east of the city of Lyon, offers a good selection of types and companies including Regional Airlines, Air Littoral, Air Inter, Brit Air, Air France and Air Transport Pyrenées, all of which can be seen and photographed from the terrace located between the two terminal spurs. A lower aspect is possible from the car park on the left of the domestic terminal building, which overlooks the associated apron. Very good ground shots at the holding point of Runway 36 are possible in the afternoon, but this depends upon the wind direction. The spot is reached via the road serving the freight centre. (Runway 18/36 (13,123ft/4,000m);Tower120.0MHz/ Approach 119.25MHz)

Marseille (Marignane)

A seasonal spectators' terrace can be found at Marseille, although from the photographic point of view it has the disadvantage of being fronted with heavily tinted glass. It can also become hot due to the lack of shade, with no facilities for the purchase of drinks. This is probably an advantage in some respects because neither are there toilets available. Most of the airline movements are provided by Air France, Air Inter and TAT, but the appearance of an Air Afrique or Air Gabon machine may make the endurance test seem worthwhile.
(Runways 14R/32L (7,774ft/2,370m), 14L/32R (11,482ft/3,500m);
Tower 119.5MHz/Approach 119.2MHz)

Metz/Nancy (Frescaty)

At the right time this airport, 3 miles (5km) southeast of the city, gives the impression of being very busy, but it is really only on the occasion of a movement generated by TAT's morning and evening schedules to Paris, Toulouse, Lyon, Marseille and Nice using ATR-42, Brasilia, Fellowship, Fokker 100 and Beech 1900. Flandre Air operates to and from Reims, but only twice daily with a Beech 1900. Since the apron extends around three sides of the terminal with the landside access allocated to the fourth, it is possible to obtain good photographs through the fence of most of the traffic. (Runways 01/19 (7,874ft/2,400m); Tower 119.7MHz/Approach 125.9MHz)

Montpellier (Fréjourges)

Mainly domestic schedules are to be found at Fréjourges, located 4 miles (6.5km) southeast of Montpellier. These are mostly operated by Air Inter and Air Littoral, the airport being the headquarters of the latter carrier. The London route flown for some years by Dan-Air prior to its demise has since been maintained by British Airways, using a 737 instead of a One-Eleven for the link with Gatwick. There are no facilities provided for the visitor, but this presents no problems because vantage points can be found. (Runways 13L/31R (8,530ft/2,600m), 13R/31L (3,280ft/1,000m); Tower 118.7MHz/Approach 119.8MHz).

Perpignan (Rivesaltes)

Best known for its pile of assorted retired airliners, Perpignan was the home of Europe Aero Services for many years. Located 4.5 miles (7km) northwest of the town, the airport receives a few scheduled services operated by Air Inter and Air Littoral during the day. Due to the scarcity of movements there is little to photograph from the terminal, although one of the night mail aircraft is often parked awaiting its next nocturnal duty. (Runways 15/33 (7,545ft/2,300m), 13/31 (4,133ft/1,260m); Tower 118.3MHz/Approach 120.75MHz)

Reims (Champagne)

The airport serves the city of Reims and the surrounding area, sharing its facilities with the military. A simple two-storey building serves as the terminal, but remains deserted for much of the time since Flandre Air provides the only scheduled services in the morning and evening. Should there by chance be a movement, it can be photographed from the side of the terminal. In any case, access to the apron should be possible, providing a member of the elusive staff can be found to authorise the request. (Runway 07/25 (8,136ft/2,480m); Tower 118.9MHz/Approach 119.8Mhz)

Strasbourg (Entzheim)

Due to the airport being jointly used by civil operators and the French Air Force, no spectators' facilities are provided. Entzheim is located 7.2 miles (12km) west of the city and possesses a modern terminal equipped with large windows overlooking the apron. Unfortunately, although most aircraft parked there can be photographed, the glass is heavily tinted. The military presence makes the local gendarmerie suspicious of

Above: The Guppies are regular sights at a number of European airports, but their home is Toulouse, the location of this shot of F-BPPA. *AJW*

cameras, especially outside the building.
(Runway 05/23 (7,874ft/2,400m);
Tower 118.7MHz/Approach 120.7MHz,
125.87MHz)

Toulouse (Blagnac)

Although the home of Airbus Industrie, very
little of its activities can be seen from the
airport terminal, which is located 6 miles
(10km) northwest of the city. In order to
reach a closer position it is necessary to
start from the N124 road near St Martin to
the south of the field. A series of right turns
eventually leads to a car park overlooking
an apron where the company's products
receive their finishing touches amidst much
clutter. Unlike the larger US manufacturers,
Airbus does not provide guided tours for the
public. The viewing area on the roof of the
terminal is usually closed, but from the
windows all scheduled movements can be
seen. These involve Air Algerie (Boeing
727/737), Air France (Airbus A320, Boeing
737, Fellowship), Air Inter (Airbus
A300/320/321/330), Air Liberte (Airbus
A300), Air Littoral (ATR-42, Brasilia,
Canadair Regional Jet), Brit Air (SAAB
SF340), Crossair (Fokker 50, SAAB 2000),
KLM (Fokker 100), Regional Airlines
(Jetstream 31), Royal Air Maroc (Boeing
727/737), Swissair (MD80), TAT (Friendship,
ATR-42, Fokker 100) and Tunis Air (Boeing
727/737).
(Runways 15R/33L11,482ft/3,500m),15L/3R
(9,842ft/3,000m);
Tower 118.1MHz/Approach 121.1MHz)

Tours (St Symphorien)

All schedules from this airport are operated
by TAT, which is not surprising since it is
the company's main base. However, any
thought that a vast selection of the carrier's
possessions will be seen can be forgotten
because the fleet is normally dispersed all
over the country. An adequate terminal
faces the apron, which can be viewed from
a balcony running along the front of the
building. Access is via the restaurant, which
seems to open irregularly, especially in the
summer months, while at ground level a wall
presents a formidable obstacle between
camera and subject.
(Runway 02/20 (7,874ft/2,400m);
Tower 118.3MHz/Approach 121.0MHz)

Germany

Berlin (Schönefeld)

Formerly in East Berlin, this airport has been
used by more western traffic since the
unification of the city. Its long runways
makes it particularly suitable for long-haul

traffic, although the airport still remains
relatively quiet compared with Tegel.
Access from the centre of the city has
slowly improved, but public transport takes
about 50min for the 12-mile (19km) journey.
The small terminal building has an excellent
rooftop terrace with no restrictions on
photography. Although the vantage point
faces south, the sun is not too much of a
problem for such activity. Schönefeld is now
the site of the German Aerospace Show,
previously held in even years at Hanover.
(Runways 07R/25L. 07L/25R;
Tower 118.3MHz, 119.12MHz/Approach
121.3MHz, 1195.5MHz, 119.7MHz)

Bremen (Neuenland)

There is a choice of vantage points around
this regional airport, located 2 miles (3.6km)
south of the city, but movements are
moderate. Lufthansa is naturally much in
evidence, while commuter carriers to be
seen are Deutsche BA and Roland Air,
although the latter's flights are operated by
Emden-based OLT. Hapag-Lloyd provides
IT services from the airport with other
German charter companies appearing from
time to time.
(Runway 09/27 (6,672ft/2,034m);
Tower 118.5MHz/Approach 125.65MHz)

Hamburg (Fuhlsbuttel)

Fuhlsbuttel lies 7.5 miles (12km) north of the
thriving city and attracts a greater number
of scheduled movements than many other
airports. Lufthansa once again
predominates, but some of the rarer
German commuter carriers are also active.
Since the extension of the terminal, charter
traffic has been allocated a separate
building, with the observation terrace on the
top floor. This facility is open daily with a
DM5 entry fee, giving good views of all
movements. A viewing area also exists at
ground level, but with limited value because
of the positioning of the jet screens. Anyone
keen on photographing lamp standards will
appreciate the efforts of those responsible
for the planting of such items around the
apron, but to most they create problems. It
is difficult not to include at least one in any
shot, unless the subject is smaller than a
737.
(Runways 05/23 (10,662ft/3,200m), 15/33
(12,024ft/3,665m);
Tower 126.85MHz, 122.7MHz/Approach
121.25MHz)

Saarbrücken (Ensheim)

Situated 7.5 miles (12km) east of the town,
Ensheim is not an airport likely to attract

many visitors, but if in the area it is worth making a slight detour to acquire a good photograph. A few scheduled services are operated, most of them to other German cities. For its size and traffic volume, the airport has a large terminal building bordering the northern edge of the apron. A small charge is made for entry on to an excellent terrace which is ideal for viewing and photography. Alternatively, the car park can become a good vantage point since it is adjacent to the light aircraft park and taxiway. Occasional appearances are made by charter flights operated by airlines such as Hapag-Lloyd.

(Runway 09/27 (6,561ft/2,000m);
Tower 118.55MHz/
Approach 129.05MHz, 119.65MHz)

Stuttgart (Echterdingen)

This is one of the larger regional airports in Germany, situated 9 miles (14km) south of the city, and as such receives a good share of scheduled traffic operated by numerous European carriers. Condor handles the majority of the charter business at Stuttgart, but Germania, Aero Lloyd, Hapag-Lloyd and Balkan also have a share. Viewing from the terminal area is not very rewarding, so ideally one should visit the end of the runways. The holding point for Runway 08

Above:
Malta's new terminal can be seen behind the ATR-72 TS-LBC operated by Tuninter and an Air Malta 737.

can be reached via a track, with good prospects for photography. If this strip is not in use, then the road leading to the village of Bernhausen is a good alternative as it passes conveniently close to the end of 26 and the nearby holding point.

(Runway 06/26 (8,366ft/2,550m);
Tower 122.7MHz/
Radar 119.2MHz)

Malta
Luqa

After an eventful wartime career, Luqa became a popular staging post for both military and civil aircraft. Various attempts were made to provide services to the airport, but eventually it was British European Airways that took over the London route with Viscounts. A new terminal was opened in 1958, but, as the level of tourism increased steadily through the years, it became unable to cope with the demand. A runway extension was completed to accommodate the larger jet types, but it was the late 1980s before approval was received for the construction of a new building. An interesting design was chosen which reflects an Arabian influence with its collection of pillars and arches. There is now ample room in the spacious premises intended to handle 2.5 million passengers per year. When the new building was formally opened in mid-1992, the original terminal was converted into a freight centre.

Air Malta naturally provides the majority of movements, its fleet linking the island with a large number of destinations. However, other carriers such as Alitalia and Swissair offer scheduled services, while European charter airlines are regular visitors. The terminal includes a spectators' gallery on the top floor overlooking the apron. While it gives good views of all the activity, unfortunately it is behind glass. This attracts a coating of sandy dust as a result of the normally dry and hot conditions, which does not help photography. Far better results can be obtained around the perimeter, especially from the fence on the southern side of the apron area. The taxiway passes close to this point and runway shots are no problem with a 200mm lens. After midday a spot on the opposite side of the runway is preferable due to the position of the sun.

(Runways 06/24 (7,800ft/2,377m), 14/32 (11,627ft/3,544m); Tower118.9MHz/
Approach 121.0MHz, 127.1MHz)

Netherlands
Eindhoven

This airport is operated jointly by the civil and military authorities. The commercial activities at Eindhoven are centred on a single-storey terminal adjacent to the Philips hangar. An open viewing area is provided to

give a good vantage point for photography. Alternatively, the layby at the threshold of Runway 22 is conveniently sited for shots of both landing and taxying aircraft. Philips' fleet also appears at intervals, but luck obviously plays a part in a visit coinciding with the timing of these events. A few charter flights also use the airport during the holiday season.
(Runway 04/22 (9,842ft/3,000m);
Tower 121.1MHz/Approach 122.45MHz)

Maastricht (Beek)

When originally conceived, Maastricht was expected to become a major centre for commercial traffic, but in reality it is a very quiet airport. Located in the Limburg region of Holland 4.5 miles (7km) northeast of the city, it is close to the Belgian and German borders but surrounded by an area which is not densely populated. Its under-used facilities handle the few scheduled services of KLM CityHopper and Air Exel Commuter, but the main activity takes place during the night when various cargo flights arrive to connect with European feeder services. Good views of the movements are possible from the hotel next to the terminal, while the terrace linking the two provides an excellent vantage point for photography.
(Runways 04/22 (8,202ft/2,500m), 07/25 (3,542ft/1,080m); Tower 119.47MHz, 119.7MHz/Approach 123.97MHz)

Rotterdam (Zestienhoven)

The close proximity of Schiphol and the convenience of the excellent ground transportation in the Netherlands has meant that Rotterdam has lost many passengers to its larger neighbour. This fact is illustrated by the 1993 statistics for Rotterdam, which show that there were 12,162 air transport movements which carried 288,655 passengers, both figures being lower than in the previous year. Nevertheless, some schedules are still maintained to the UK by KLM CityHopper (Fellowships), VLM (Fokker 50) and CityFlyer Express (ATR-42, Short SD3-60). Until early 1994, Flexair operated a Dornier 228 on the London City route, but following the company's demise VLM took over the route, at the same time offering connections with its UK domestic service to Liverpool (since withdrawn). A spacious modern terminal was built at Rotterdam in 1971, alongside which is a viewing terrace. From this point photographs can easily be obtained but, depending upon the stand used, a parked aircraft can obscure the scene until it departs. On the opposite side

of the building another spectators' area overlooks the general aviation apron.
(Runway 06/24 (7,217ft/2,200m);
Tower 118.2MHz/Approach 121.2MHz)

Portugal
Faro

The airport offers the usual selection of European charter airlines, but with good opportunities for viewing and photography. The terminal has an excellent rooftop gallery, while other vantage points can be found around the perimeter. One such position is found along a track which runs parallel with the runway off the road to Praia de Faro. Sufficient concrete blocks are in position to enable even those with a height disadvantage to obtain good shots over the fence. (Runway 11/29 (7,874ft/2,400m);
Tower 118.2MHz/Approach 119.4MHz)

Lisbon (Portela de Sacavem)

Located 4.5 miles (7km) north of the city, the airport attracts few airlines that cannot be seen elsewhere in less difficult conditions. The original viewing gallery is closed, but there is a terrace above the domestic facility which can be used. Photography is not easy through the glass due to the reflections and distance from the subject. There is a charge levied, but this gives access all day. The ends of the runways are accessible, with 03 providing landing and taxying shots of reasonable quality. Photography may produce some hostile reactions because of the presence of the military.
(Runways 03/21 (12,483ft/3,805m), 18/36 (7,874ft/2,400m);
Tower 118.1MHz/Approach 119.1MHz, 119.7MHz, 120.6MHz)

Spain
Barcelona

This airport has seen a steady decline in the amount of charter traffic handled compared with the 1970s when the region was very popular with tourists. Scheduled movements now provide most of the activity and are created mainly by Iberia, Viva and Aviaco. Other European carriers also visit Barcelona regularly, including British Airways, KLM, SABENA, Lufthansa, Air Portugal, SAS, Alitalia, Air France and Swissair. The choice of the city for the 1992 Olympic Games brought considerable business to the airport and also prompted the construction of a new terminal building.
(Runways 02/20 (8,923ft/2,720m), 07/25

(11,000ft/3,353m);
Tower 118.1MHz/Approach 124.7MHz)

Ibiza

As a popular holiday island, Ibiza is busy with IT traffic from all over Europe, but particularly from Britain and Germany. There are good views of the apron through the tinted windows of the new terminal's domestic departure area, this building having relegated the original structure to general aviation usage. A track runs from the airport complex alongside the fence towards the threshold of Runway 07, a spot offering a useful vantage point for landing shots. The approach path to Runway 25 passes over Playa den Bossa, where several hotels are conveniently situated for viewing the many movements at close quarters, albeit at the expense of sleep. (Runway 06/24 (9,186ft/2,800m);
Tower 118.5MHz/Approach 119.8MHz)

Madrid (Barajas)

Although millions of holidaymakers visit Spain, few of them actually include the capital in their itinerary. It is, after all, some distance from the nearest beach. Likewise the airport, which is located 10 miles (16km) northeast of the city, is not a place normally included in a tour of such establishments. However, excellent views of the proceedings can be obtained from the first floor of the domestic terminal, although photography has to be through tinted glass and is a pursuit forbidden by the authorities. Shots of the various aircraft on the cargo apron are possible from outside the international terminal, often including specimens operated by some unusual companies due to Spain's association with South America. However, in view of the aversion to cameras of the local law officers, it is prudent to exercise discretion and go elsewhere. (Runways 01/19 (12,139ft/3,700m), 15/33 (13,451ft/4,100m);
Tower 118.15MHz/
Approach 119.9MHz, 120.0MHz)

Malaga

A large, modern terminal handles the vast number of visitors to this region of Spain, most of them arriving on charter flights operated by the familiar European companies. There is no official viewing area provided, but departing passengers have the benefit of large windows overlooking both apron, taxiway and runway. Although the glass is lightly tinted, this has no detrimental effect on photographs. However, shots are best obtained from the perimeter fence on the opposite side of the field, a 300mm lens being preferable for all but the largest types. It is necessary to use a car to reach this vantage point via a series of right turns after leaving the terminal. Eventually, the road becomes a track, usefully at a higher level than the fence, thereby assisting photography over the top. (Runway 14/32 (10,500ft/3,200m);
Tower 118.15MHz/Approach 118.45MHz, 123.95MHz)

Menorca (Mahon)

This island is the quietest of the main Balearics group, a fact reflected by the number of movements at the airport. Nevertheless, the original terminal was inadequate, so the Spanish authorities replaced it with a spacious building more suited to the task. In the process all sight of the apron has been lost from within and no longer does the departure lounge have an open-air section overlooking the proceedings. A vantage point to the right of the terminal gives a view of some of the stands, but, strangely, photography tends to be discouraged by the local security staff. A less obvious spot can be found at the end of Runway 01, but this involves a car and a journey fit only for mules, so whether the effort is worthwhile is debatable. (Runway 01/19 (7.700ft/2,350m); Tower 119.65MHz)

Sweden
Stockholm (Bromma)

Bromma was formally opened by King Gustav V on 23 May 1936, followed by the launch of international schedules on 1 July. Services were quickly introduced by Lufthansa, KLM, SABENA, Air France and British Airways, the latter using DH86s on the London route. Thereafter, the airport continued to handle all of Stockholm's commercial traffic, but in the 1960s the international operations were moved to the newly completed Arlanda, with domestic movements joining them in October 1983. Noise and lack of space were the main reasons for the moves, leaving Bromma to handle the not inconsiderable general aviation traffic.

During the war the Swedish airport had performed an important function by maintaining a vital link between Sweden and Scotland, a sector fraught with danger for the slow transports involved. In 1942 the occasional use of a Mosquito brought a request from BOAC for some modified specimens to take over the route. This was approved, resulting in the frequent sight of the advanced British design parked beside German airliners on the neutral apron at Bromma.

With the availability of the quiet BAe 146, Malmö Aviation applied for a licence to resume scheduled services from the airport, only 5 miles (8km) from the city centre compared with Arlanda's 25 miles (40km). Surprisingly, the local population were much in favour of the revival, especially since the proposed service was to use London City as the UK terminal, while domestic links with Malmö and Gothenburg were also planned. Before the start-up in 1992, the airport authorities had to re-provide facilities long-removed such as check-in desks, immigration and security devices. A restaurant had to be converted into a departure lounge on the upper floor, while the domestic gates remained at ground level. All the necessary work was completed in time for the inaugurals, but, unfortunately, after a relatively short time the international service was suspended pending a reorganisation within the company.

There are no official viewing facilities provided, but good views are possible through the fence adjacent to the terminal building. Requests for access to the light aircraft parking area are also sometimes received sympathetically. (Runway 12/30 (5,863ft/1,787m); Tower 118.1MHz, 119.4MHz/Approach 120.15MHz)

Switzerland
Basle/Mulhouse

Located 3.5 miles (5.6km) northwest of the city, the airport was built on land leased from the French due to the lack of a suitable site in Switzerland. This resulted in a fenced corridor to carry the access road from Basle to the left side of the terminal and other Swiss-operated facilities. The right-hand section of the building is in French hands and it is not possible to cross over the boundary. For this reason it is always best to approach the complex from the direction of Switzerland since the more interesting areas are then accessible.

A balcony is provided along the front of the terminal and is reached via a lift to the restaurant floor. The terrace is also divided in the middle with a wire fence discouraging infiltration into the French sector. Entry tickets costing SFr1 are obtainable from a machine positioned adjacent to the security check point, at which the occupant usually expresses an interest in camera bags. Opening hours appear to vary, but it would seem to be accessible fairly consistently in the afternoons. Unfortunately, the sun is not in the best position for photography after midday, but due to the vantage point's elevation, it is by no means impossible to acquire reasonable shots.

Basle/Mulhouse is the headquarters of Crossair, with the company using the airport as a hub in its scheduled network. All types in the airline's fleet appear at some time during the day, with British Airways and Swissair also having a presence. African Safari Airways is resident, its DC-10-30 frequently to be seen during a lengthy turnround. The possibility of photographing aircraft serving the French section depends largely on the wind direction and the runway in use. Basle has always been a popular destination for charter traffic, the passengers transferring to coaches for their onward journey into the Alps or even beyond. A considerable number of interesting company aircraft either visit Basle regularly for maintenance or are based at the airport. (Runways 08/26 (5,249ft/1,600m), 16/34 (12,795ft/3,900m); Tower 118.3MHz/Approach 119.35MHz)

Berne (Belp)

It is often overlooked that Berne is the capital of Switzerland, with many under the impression that either Zürich or Geneva contains the country's administrators. In fact, the airport does nothing to dispel this belief. Neatly arranged in a valley with some formidable hills and mountains nearby, the airport possesses a single hard runway together with a parallel grass strip. The site is situated 1,673ft (510m) above sea level, which produces weight limitations for airliners in hot weather conditions. It is operated by Alpar, a company formed in 1929 by the State and City of Berne to provide scheduled air services. However, in February 1947 the airline's operations were taken over by Swissair despite an intensive campaign to remain an independent carrier. Nowadays, the company concentrates on its airport responsibilities, together with general handling and flying school activities.

Since 1980 Crossair has provided the majority of the scheduled movements, which now total 20 every weekday. Air Engiadina, Arcus-Air and Euro Direct together add a further 14 services to and from Belp, which has highlighted the need for some expansion. The present facilities are certainly modest, and the small, single-storey accommodation is due to be replaced by larger premises. This also applies to the tower located adjacent to the terminal, but the reconstruction programme is not due for completion until the end of 1999. It would also be advantageous to extend the runway since there is ample space for such an undertaking. However, the contract held by Alpar until 2016 does not allow any lengthening work because it would encourage an increase in activity, with the resultant noise problems.

The airport is open between 07.00hrs and 22.00hrs, but there is a special dispensation for a service known as the 'early bird', which departs to Basle at 06.30hrs in order to connect with a wide range of European flights. Similarly, the occasional unavoidable late arrival after the official closing time is tolerated, the last programmed movement being the 21.55hrs Crossair flight from Basle. A well positioned grass enclosure enables photographs to be taken of movements on the taxiway, apron or runway, each including the scenic background.

(Runway 14/32 (4,300ft/1,310m);
Tower 118.9MHz/Approach 124.35MHz)

United Kingdom
Glasgow (Abbotsinch)

Since taking over from Renfrew in May 1966, Abbotsinch has undergone considerable development. It became the terminal for the UK's first shuttle service in 1975, when regular links were introduced to London by British Airways, but Prestwick remained the transatlantic terminal for Glasgow. Phase one of a major expansion programme, begun in 1987, was declared open in June 1992. While this increased the size of the accommodation, thereby encouraging airlines to introduce long-haul services, the second phase includes a new international pier built to the west of the terminal. It is a two-storey building with the capability of handling six wide-bodied aircraft on stands complete with airbridges. Once operational in 1995, this stage will raise the airport's capacity from 5.5 million to 10 million passengers per year. Unfortunately, the airport suffered a setback in the autumn of 1994 when several airlines announced the reduction or suspension of services due to poor yields. There are no viewing facilities provided, but vantage points exist around the perimeter.

(Runways 05/23 (8,720ft/2,658m), 10/28 (3,570ft/1,088m);
Tower 118.8MHz/Approach 119.1MHz)

Below:
The restored DC-3 SE-CFP displays its SAS livery at Bromma. *AJW*

Index

Top:
Viva operates to a number of Spanish destinations from Heathrow. The Boeing 737-300 EC-FLF is seen taxying on to its stand alongside EC-FHR. *AJW*
Above:
Aeroflot uses Tu-154s such as RA-85769 for its scheduled services into Zurich. *AJW*